OPPOSING VIEWPOINTS® SERIES

The Culture of Beauty

Other Books of Related Interest:

"Congress shall make
no law . . . abridging
the freedom of speech,
or of the press."

First Amendment to the U.S. Constitution

The basic foundation of our democracy is the First Amendment guarantee of freedom of expression. The Opposing Viewpoints Series is dedicated to the concept of this basic freedom and the idea that it is more important to practice it than to enshrine it.

OPPOSING
VIEWPOINTS®
SERIES

The Culture of Beauty

Roman Espejo, Book Editor

GREENHAVEN PRESS
A part of Gale, Cengage Learning

GALE
CENGAGE Learning™

Detroit • New York • San Francisco • New Haven, Conn • Waterville, Maine • London

Christine Nasso, *Publisher*
Elizabeth Des Chenes, *Managing Editor*

For more information, contact:
Greenhaven Press
27500 Drake Rd.
Farmington Hills, MI 48331-3535
Or you can visit our Internet site at gale.cengage.com

For product information and technology assistance, contact us at

Gale Customer Support, 1-800-877-4253
For permission to use material from this text or product, submit all requests online at www.cengage.com/permissions

Further permissions questions can be emailed to permissionrequest@cengage.com

Articles in Greenhaven Press anthologies are often edited for length to meet page require-ments. In addition, original titles of these works are changed to clearly present the main thesis and to explicitly indicate the author's opinion. Every effort is made to ensure that Greenhaven Press accurately reflects the original intent of the authors. Every effort has been made to trace the owners of copyrighted material.

Cover Image copyright © Purestock/Florian Franke.

LIBRARY OF CONGRESS CATALOGING-IN-PUBLICATION DATA

The culture of beauty / Roman Espejo, book editor.
    p. cm. -- (Opposing viewpoints)
    Includes bibliographical references and index.
    ISBN 978-0-7377-4508-5 (hardcover)
    ISBN 978-0-7377-4509-2 (pbk.)
    1. Feminine beauty (Aesthetics)--Juvenile literature. 2. Aesthetics--Social aspects--Juvenile literature. I. Espejo, Roman, 1977-
    HQ1219.C83 2010
    306.4'613--dc22

                                                                        2009033675

Printed in the United States of America
  2 3 4 5 6   15 14 13 12 11

FD186

Contents

Why Consider Opposing Viewpoints?

> *"The only way in which a human being can make some approach to knowing the whole of a subject is by hearing what can be said about it by persons of every variety of opinion and studying all modes in which it can be looked at by every character of mind. No wise man ever acquired his wisdom in any mode but this."*
>
> John Stuart Mill

In our media-intensive culture it is not difficult to find differing opinions. Thousands of newspapers and magazines and dozens of radio and television talk shows resound with differing points of view. The difficulty lies in deciding which opinion to agree with and which "experts" seem the most credible. The more inundated we become with differing opinions and claims, the more essential it is to hone critical reading and thinking skills to evaluate these ideas. Opposing Viewpoints books address this problem directly by presenting stimulating debates that can be used to enhance and teach these skills. The varied opinions contained in each book examine many different aspects of a single issue. While examining these conveniently edited opposing views, readers can develop critical thinking skills such as the ability to compare and contrast authors' credibility, facts, argumentation styles, use of persuasive techniques, and other stylistic tools. In short, the Opposing Viewpoints Series is an ideal way to attain the higher-level thinking and reading skills so essential in a culture of diverse and contradictory opinions.

In addition to providing a tool for critical thinking, Opposing Viewpoints books challenge readers to question their own strongly held opinions and assumptions. Most people form their opinions on the basis of upbringing, peer pressure, and personal, cultural, or professional bias. By reading carefully balanced opposing views, readers must directly confront new ideas as well as the opinions of those with whom they disagree. This is not to simplistically argue that everyone who reads opposing views will—or should—change his or her opinion. Instead, the series enhances readers' understanding of their own views by encouraging confrontation with opposing ideas. Careful examination of others' views can lead to the readers' understanding of the logical inconsistencies in their own opinions, perspective on why they hold an opinion, and the consideration of the possibility that their opinion requires further evaluation.

Evaluating Other Opinions

To ensure that this type of examination occurs, Opposing Viewpoints books present all types of opinions. Prominent spokespeople on different sides of each issue as well as well-known professionals from many disciplines challenge the reader. An additional goal of the series is to provide a forum for other, less known, or even unpopular viewpoints. The opinion of an ordinary person who has had to make the decision to cut off life support from a terminally ill relative, for example, may be just as valuable and provide just as much insight as a medical ethicist's professional opinion. The editors have two additional purposes in including these less known views. One, the editors encourage readers to respect others' opinions—even when not enhanced by professional credibility. It is only by reading or listening to and objectively evaluating others' ideas that one can determine whether they are worthy of consideration. Two, the inclusion of such viewpoints encourages the important critical thinking skill of objectively evaluating an author's credentials and bias. This evaluation will illuminate an author's reasons for taking a particular stance on an issue and will aid in readers' evaluation of the author's ideas.

It is our hope that these books will give readers a deeper understanding of the issues debated and an appreciation of the complexity of even seemingly simple issues when good and honest people disagree. This awareness is particularly important in a democratic society such as ours in which people enter into public debate to determine the common good. Those with whom one disagrees should not be regarded as enemies but rather as people whose views deserve careful examination and may shed light on one's own.

Thomas Jefferson once said that "difference of opinion leads to inquiry, and inquiry to truth." Jefferson, a broadly educated man, argued that "if a nation expects to be ignorant and free . . . it expects what never was and never will be." As individuals and as a nation, it is imperative that we consider the opinions of others and examine them with skill and discernment. The Opposing Viewpoints Series is intended to help readers achieve this goal.

David L. Bender and Bruno Leone,
Founders

Introduction

> *"Some people call her a beauty queen. We call her a scholar."*
>
> *—Web site of the*
> *Miss America Pageant*
>
> *"All women were made to believe they were inferior because they couldn't measure up to Miss America beauty standards."*
>
> *—Jo Freeman,*
> *feminist scholar*

From 1941 to 1977, the Miss Subways pageant in New York City challenged mainstream notions of beauty in the United States. Two minority women—an African American and an Asian American of Chinese heritage—won Miss Subways, in 1948 and 1949, respectively, more than thirty years before Miss America chose its first African American winner. Holders of the Miss Subways title also defied categorization and stereotypes. Identical twins Mary and Kathryn Keeler were simultaneously anointed in 1958—how to tell them apart: "Mary smokes, Kathryn doesn't."[1] Eleanor Nash, a Miss Subways during 1960, was a clerk for the Federal Bureau of Investigation (FBI) and belonged to a firearms organization, her poster aptly describing her as "young, beautiful, and expert with a rifle."[2]

Indeed, the eligibility requirements for the Miss Subways pageant were simple (in general, female residents of New York City who commuted via subway), and minorities had lobbied the modeling agency that determined its nominees and winners from the start. Wrote one activist in a letter to the editor, "This is not just a question of getting a Negro girl chosen as

Miss Subways, or even to get started getting modeling jobs open to Negro women in agencies that discriminate at present. This can be the beginning of getting pictures of Negros in our magazines, newspapers, subway ads, etc."[3] As a matter of fact, Thelma Porter, the first African American Miss Subways, graced the pages of minority magazines and newspapers across the nation and was honored at a reception by the late Thurgood Marshall, the first African American justice to serve on the U.S. Supreme Court.

Since its origins in New Jersey's Atlantic City almost nine decades ago, the American beauty pageant has served as an intersection of women's issues and civil rights. For instance, Margaret Gorman, crowned the first Miss America in 1921, represented "the type of womanhood America needs—strong, red-blooded, able to shoulder the responsibilities of homemaking and motherhood,"[4] according to labor union leader Samuel Gompers. However, women's and religious groups condemned its contestants' coiffed hairstyles and skin-baring ensembles, and their efforts shut down the pageant in 1928, until it eventually returned in the mid-1930s.

In the following decades, events at the Miss America Pageant reflected changing cultural mores. In 1945, Bess Myerson became the first Jewish American to seize the title and campaigned with the catchphrase "You Can't Be Beautiful and Hate" after encountering anti-semitic backlash. Five years later, in 1950, a seeming blow for women's rights took place at the pageant. That year's winner, Yolande Betbeze, declined to pose in a swimsuit after being crowned the winner. Miss America's board of directors supported her decision. The move, nonetheless, incensed Catalina Swimwear, a major sponsor of the pageant, and the company withdrew and went on to establish its rival, Miss USA, as well as the Miss Teen USA and Miss Universe contests. On the other hand, the Miss America organization credits Betbeze with the pageant's greater recognition of scholarship and achievement.

With the rise of feminism and the advent of the sexual liberation movement, women's rights organizations and activists ushered a critical view of beauty pageants in the 1960s and 1970s. At the Miss America pageant in 1968, protestors circulated the infamous brochure *No More Miss America*, its ten points outlining alleged objectification, racism, commercialism, and imposition of double standards. The effects of such allegations saw, in 1973, Miss America's crowning of Rebecca Ann King, a law student who openly supported the legalization of abortion. *Newsweek* even asked, "Is the new Miss America a feminist?"[5] (In her own words, "probably semi."[6]) Ten years later, the anointing of the pageant's first African American winner, actress and singer Vanessa Williams, was a major, but short-lived, milestone for black women in the 1980s, as Williams suddenly resigned amid a photo scandal.

In contemporary America, Miss USA has moved to the forefront of beauty pageant issues and controversies. Tara Connor, Miss USA 2006, was nearly dethroned because of allegations of underage drinking, cocaine use, and other indiscretions. A year later, Laura Upton, a contestant in Miss Teen USA, was derided for her incoherent response to a question on education. And in 2009, Carrie Prejean, first runner-up to Miss USA that year, claimed that she had lost the national title and was fired from her post as Miss California USA because of her views against gay marriage, which she had expressed during a portion of the Miss USA competition. As for Miss Subways, the pageant was revived—as "Ms. Subways"—for one year in 2004. Actress Caroline Sanchez-Bernat, who had previously participated in a piece of group performance art while riding a subway car, won the title and appeared in a citywide campaign endorsing commuter safety and kindness.

Pageants are but one aspect of the culture that surrounds beauty. It dwells in expected and unexpected places, from a model's flawless face on a magazine page to, purportedly, the cutthroat job market. This anthology, *Opposing Viewpoints: The Culture of Beauty*, presents contrasting perspectives on this topic in the following chapters: What Are the Standards of Beauty? How Do Images of Beauty Affect Society? Should People Strive for Beauty? What Are the Effects of the Beauty and Fashion Industries? The authors—researchers and advocates, women and men—investigate how beauty affects the eye of the beholder.

Notes

1. Anthony Ramirez, *New York Times*, October 26, 2004.
2. Anthony Ramirez, *New York Times*, October 26, 2004.
3. Jennifer 8. Lee, *New York Times*, April 21, 2009.
4. missamerica.org (accessed June 22, 2009).
5. Patricia Bradley, *Mass Media and the Shaping of American Feminism, 1963–1975*, 2003.
6. Patricia Bradley, *Mass Media and the Shaping of American Feminism, 1963–1975*, 2003.

OPPOSING
VIEWPOINTS®
SERIES

CHAPTER 1

What Are the Standards of Beauty?

Chapter Preface

At the University of Texas at Austin and Harvard University, researchers surveyed 354,000 British and American literary works from the sixteenth to the eighteenth centuries and three canons of ancient Asian literature (two from India, one from China) to answer an age-old question: What makes a woman beautiful? Their conclusion: A small waist. Collecting references in the texts to womanly erogenous zones—including the breasts, thighs, and buttocks—the researchers claim that appraisals of a small waist outnumbered them all. Romantic and erotic phrases like "as little as a wand" and "beholden to her lovely waist" occurred in the English-language samples sixty-five times, compared with sixteen mentions of the breasts, two of the thighs, and another two of the buttocks. This preference was more pronounced in the Asian samples, according to the researchers. In the two Indian classics, the waist notched up thirty-five mentions, nine more than the breasts, thighs, and other aspects of the female form. As for the Chinese sample, depictions of a slim midriff appeared seventeen times, while the legs were mentioned just once and the rest completely ignored. "In spite of variation in the description of beauty," the researchers state, "the marker of health and fertility—a small waist—has always been an invariant symbol of feminine beauty."[1]

Still, in other instances, the hourglass figure is not the preferred trait. The nape of a woman's neck, as seen with the distinct makeup of the geisha, is considered highly sensual in Japan. And, while agonizing and debilitating, female foot binding was practiced in China for centuries to achieve the desired and idealized "golden lotus," a heel-to-toe length of about three inches. In the following chapter, the authors debate whether the ideals of beauty are biological, cultural, or comparative.

Notes

1. Richard Ingham, Agence France-Presse, January 10, 2007.

> *"Believing beauty to be in the eye of the beholder isn't exactly wrong, but research suggests that there are some universal standards to attractiveness that everyone seems to apply."*

The Standards of Beauty Are Universal

Elizabeth Quil

Elizabeth Quil is news editor of Science News. *In the following viewpoint, Quil proposes that facial beauty may signal universally desired traits to potential partners, such as health, fertility, and genetic fitness. According to her, researchers using computer technology to isolate certain facial characteristics have discovered that symmetry is not as essential as previously thought. In fact, features lacking distinctness are linked to a strong immune system, Quil suggests. Furthermore, the author adds that sexually dimorphic traits (e.g., high cheekbones and large eyes for females, a prominent jaw for males), as well as how facial movements differ between the sexes, support the idea that femininity and masculinity are important to standards of attractiveness.*

Elizabeth Quil, "It's Written All Over Your Face: To Potential Mates, Your Mug May Reveal More Than You Think," *Science News*, vol. 175, January 17, 2009, pp. 24–28. Copyright © 2009 by Service Science. Republished with permission of Service Science, conveyed through Copyright Clearance Center, Inc.

As you read, consider the following questions:

1. How does Quil describe the "golden proportion"?

2. According to the viewpoint, what facial movements indicate femininity?

3. As stated by Quil, what male traits do women find attractive at their most fertile time of the month?

Eye candy might more appropriately be called brain candy. Seeing a pretty face is like eating a piece of oh-so-sweet chocolate—for the brain, if not for the stomach. In fact, attractive faces activate the same reward circuitry in the brain as food, drugs, and money. For humans, there is something captivating and unforgettable about the arrangement of two balls, a point, and a horizontal slit on the front of the head.

The power of faces isn't lost on psychologists. "Faces are interesting because they impart so much information—expression, attention—and these interact with facial beauty," says Anthony Little of the University of Stifling in Scotland.

So it's no surprise that making faces attractive is big business. Each year, Americans spend more than $13 billion on cosmetic surgery and tens of billions on cosmetics and beauty aids.

But while facial improvements leave those who subscribe to them with a healthy glow and the illusion of youth—subtracting a few years can bump you up a few notches on the hot-or-not barometer—studies of attractiveness have tended to leave the scientists who undertake them with puzzled looks, gray hairs, and wrinkles.

Recently, though, researchers seeking to unmask the essence of facial attractiveness have been using computer technology to isolate the characteristics long rumored to underlie beauty. New methods reveal that averageness, or a lack of distinctness, makes someone more appealing while facial symmetry doesn't automatically make a knockout, as most people believe. Features that make a man look manly or a woman feminine can trump both averageness and symmetry, but only sometimes. And studies of faces in motion support the idea that femininity and masculinity are important to attractiveness.

Researchers have also started focusing on why faces are attractive, not just what makes them so. Attractiveness may signal good genes and a good mate. A new study links averageness to diversity in the major histocompatibility complex—a cluster of genes that plays a major role in the immune system. And brain-imaging studies are poised to capture how the brain responds to potential cues to genetic fitness.

Seeking (to Define) Beauty

Believing beauty to be in the eye of the beholder isn't exactly wrong, but research suggests that there are some universal standards to attractiveness that everyone seems to apply.

"When you look at what people find attractive, it is consistent across cultures," says evolutionary psychologist Hanne Lie of the University of Western Australia in Perth. "We have some innate or hardwired beauty detector."

Most attractiveness research has focused on three aspects of a pretty visage—averageness, symmetry, and sexual dimorphism.

Early research into these three characteristics relied on photographs and a ruler, so it was difficult to separate the characteristics from each other. Nowadays computer technology has revealed a deeper understanding of beauty.

"The huge benefit of computer graphics," Little says, "is in manipulating one thing and one thing only." For example, he says, it is possible to take any face shape and make it perfectly symmetrical. It is possible to mark points to determine average positions, such as the height of the ears, length of the nose, and distances between the eyes. It's even possible to morph faces to accentuate masculine or feminine features. Isolating such characteristics has revealed new complexities to how averageness, symmetry, and sexual dimorphism help define beauty.

Averageness, one researcher quipped, could account for as much as 85 percent of good looks. Here, average does not mean dull or boring, but rather nondescript, lacking distinct or dramatic features. In the late 1870s, Sir Francis Galton combined photos of men convicted of serious crimes to develop an image of the prototypical criminal's face. He found the composite image—with its smoothed out features and absence of irregularities—surprisingly attractive. More than a century later, in the early 1990s, psychologist Judith Langlois, now at the University of Texas at Austin, and her colleagues confirmed that blended faces are more attractive than the originals. (Averaged faces are also preferred by infants; babies stare at composites longer.)

Symmetry as a feature of attractiveness dates back to Plato's day. He believed the "golden proportion" was the key to a good-looking face. The width of the ideal face would be two-thirds its length and the nose no longer than the distance between the eyes. Modern research suggests that symmetry judgments depend on how well one half of the face reflects the other, Little says. Asymmetry makes a face look a bit off; the two sides don't quite match. "Essentially, it's wonkiness," he says.

And anyone who has gawked at a supermodel with big eyes and high cheekbones or the prominent jaw of a soap opera hunk knows that these beauties bring something else to the mirror. Sexually dimorphic characteristics—meaning those that make someone very masculine or very feminine—can take a face from beautiful to, well, sexy.

Average Versus Distinct Features

Fully understanding facial beauty requires studying how these three facial characteristics relate and interact. Averageness is attractive, says Lisa DeBruine, an experimental psychologist at the University of Aberdeen in Scotland. But, she says, when it comes to some key features, such as big eyes and small chins in women, being distinctly nonaverage (being very feminine) can be better. Distinctness is, by default, thought of as bad because, she says, "there are more ways to be nonaverage and ugly than there are ways to be nonaverage and beautiful."

In a series of studies, researchers including Little and Steven Gangestad of the University of New Mexico in Albuquerque also found that symmetrical faces have attractive features independent of their symmetry. Symmetry was attractive in male faces, for instance, but women shown only half of an attractive male face still found the face attractive, Little and colleagues reported in 2001 in the *Proceedings of the Royal Society*.

A further study, published by Little on May 7 [2009] in *PLoS ONE*, suggests that symmetry goes up and down with sexually dimorphic features in Europeans, African hunter-gatherers, and in nonhuman primates. Symmetrical males had more masculine features and symmetrical females had more feminine features. Gangestad has shown that symmetry and masculinity vary together in men—as one increases, the other does too, suggesting the two characteristics point to some unknown underlying quality. So, perhaps, symmetry is important not on its own, but as a proxy for other characteristics—identified or not yet identified, researchers suggest.

Other missing elements in evaluating beauty have begun to emerge with the use of new technology. Video techniques have allowed for dynamic rather than static interpretations of beauty.

"Real faces move," says Edward Morrison of the University of Bristol in England. "If you show someone a moving face, they can recognize it quicker. There is more information."

And it turns out that how faces move may contribute to how good they look. In a 2007 paper in *Evolution and Human*

Behavior, Morrison reported that more of the movements known to be indicators of femininity—blinking, nodding, and head tilting—made women's faces more attractive to male and female volunteers.

"Movement can convey important meanings," Morrison says. "If that person likes you or doesn't. If that person is being aggressive. If the person is being flirtatious. The face can start to convey these kinds of things."

The findings echo results from studies of static faces, supporting the conclusion that sexual dimorphism is important in evaluating women's faces, and less important in evaluating men's faces, which tend to move less.

Little says that while scientists are slowly finding all the pieces, fitting them together remains a challenge. "As far as the actual relative weight of these things," he says, "I don't know whether we have a good handle on what is most important."

Designed to Impress

If the first goal is to find out what is attractive, the next is to understand why. More than triggering mere identity, facial features can reveal the sex, age, and race of their owners. Movement can indicate mood and interest. And clues to personality may also be present, or at least people may think they are. (Studies have shown that voters believe baby faces suggest incompetence while jutting chins and angular noses are clues to capability in candidates. Another study suggests that people think baby faces make more honest CEOs [chief executive officers].)

But faces are far subtler vessels still. If a male peacock can show a female his fitness by growing colorful feathers, maybe humans can, more subtly, reveal their fitness with the features on their faces. And people may subconsciously pick up on the cues that identify a good mate.

Under this assumption, masculine features may signal a strong and protective partner, while feminine features com-

The Science of Beauty

Studies have shown that there is surprising agreement about what makes a face attractive. Symmetry is at the core, along with youthfulness; clarity or smoothness of skin; and vivid color, say, in the eyes and hair. There is little dissent among people of different cultures, ethnicities, races, ages and gender.

Yet, like the many other attempts to use objective principles or even mathematical formulas to define beauty, this software program [which alters a photo based on ideal facial proportions] raises what psychologists, philosophers and feminists say are complex, even disturbing, questions about the perception of beauty and a beauty ideal.

To what extent is beauty quantifiable? Does a supposedly scientific definition merely reflect the ideal of the moment, built from the images of pop culture and the news media?

Sarah Kershaw,
"The Sum of Your Facial Parts,"
The New York Times, *October 9, 2008.*

municate youth and fertility. Asymmetries would signal underlying developmental instability. An individual's genetic profile would also contribute to averageness.

Lie and her colleagues Gill Rhodes and Leigh Simmons, both also of the University of Western Australia, connected averageness, genetic profile, and attractiveness in a recent study. In male faces, attractiveness signaled diversity within the major histocompatibility complex [MHC], the team reports in the October 2008 *Evolution*.

This cluster of 128 genes and surrounding genetic material plays an important role in the immune system. The genes encode molecules on the cell surface that recognize self from nonself and detect pathogens and parasites. In rhesus macaques, diversity in the MHC has been linked to reproductive success. And female fat-tailed dwarf lemurs have been shown to prefer males with greater MHC diversity.

Lie looked at genetic diversity in 80 men and 80 women whose faces were rated on a 10-point attractiveness scale by volunteers. The researchers found that those rated most attractive showed greater diversity in the MHC. Taking the study a step further, Lie and her colleagues linked averageness to diversity in the MHC for the first time. More diversity means a better mate, the thinking goes. Presumably, more variation in the MHC will help a person fight off diseases and infection, and a potential mate would pass on this fitness advantage to future offspring.

Attracted to Health

A number of other studies have attempted to link the features that make a face attractive to perceived, and, in a few cases, actual health. A 2000 study by Rhodes and Leslie Zebrowitz of Brandeis University in Waltham, Mass., showed that volunteers rated people with more symmetrical and more average faces as appearing healthier. Faces of 17-year-olds that were rated as distinct were associated with poor past health records. And a study in 2004 linked apparent health of facial skin to attractiveness. Some studies have hinted that attractiveness is related to longevity, body mass index, and even semen quality.

Most intriguing to Little and others are studies revealing that when women are at the most fertile time in their monthly cycle—when male quality might be most important to them reproductively—they are more interested in men with masculine and symmetrical faces.

"Women prefer all sorts of things when they are ovulating," Gangestad says. "More masculine faces, more masculine voices, more muscular bodies. Taller men. More dominant men. Certain scents."

At other times, researchers suspect, women might be interested in other traits—like a man's nurturing ability or willingness to hang around and raise children.

"There are trade-offs," Gangestad says. For example, "more masculine men may be less reliable partners."

Presumably women are more tuned in to indicators of quality when they are able to conceive, so researchers say studying those women might provide the best clues to what makes a man attractive and why. Studying the women at other times may explain the factors beyond attractiveness that contribute to choosing a life partner—why, for example, women don't always just go for the more manly man.

"Facial features don't tell us everything," Gangestad says, "but we know they tell us something."

DeBruine says studies reveal that individuals' preferences for faces are not arbitrary, but vary in specific, systematic ways. New research shows that men's preferences also change depending on their hormone levels. Working with DeBruine, Little, and other colleagues, Lisa Welling of Aberdeen found that when men have higher levels of salivary testosterone, they prefer more feminine faces. If high testosterone is a signal of better quality, men with such levels may know that they can better compete in the good-female-getting game. Men with lower levels may look for lower quality (less feminine) women. "Maybe I think Brad Pitt is the most attractive mate possible, but I am not going to win him," DeBruine says. "It is not a good strategy for me to set my sights on him." The study, which appeared online in *Hormones and Behavior* [August 2008], and others suggest that attractiveness preferences may depend on a person's own perceived attractiveness.

So your personal preferences aren't entirely personal. Studies out of Aberdeen suggest that, in addition to your hormonal profile and how attractive you think you are, how much someone looks like you and how much attention they pay you can influence just how attracted you are, in quite predictable ways.

Exploring the Universal Standards

But here's the catch. Caring about specific features is one thing, articulating those preferences is another. Even people who consistently rate symmetrical faces as attractive, for example, have trouble identifying symmetrical faces. People just know an attractive face when they see it.

So does at least one computer. Eytan Ruppin of Tel Aviv University in Israel and colleagues have trained a computer to recognize what humans would rate as an attractive female face. The machine, described in January 2008 in *Vision Research*, automatically extracted measurements of facial features from raw images rated by study participants for attractiveness. It considered thousands of features and then condensed them. Then it went to work on a fresh set of faces. The computer predicted attractiveness in these new faces in line with human preferences.

Even more intriguing, the computer replicated at least one human bias. Symmetry studies often involve taking the right side of a face and mirror imaging it to create a full face or taking the left side and doing the same. Humans show a surprising bias; in two-thirds of cases, they prefer left-left images (from the point of view of the onlooker). Somehow, this bias must have been embedded in the original rankings the computer received because it also preferred these faces. But no one is sure why or how.

Though replicating human ratings is a fun exercise in artificial intelligence, Ruppin says a computer can't help scientists understand what people find attractive. "It says what is in the mind of the computer, not the mind of a human."

Some researchers are, in fact, turning to the human mind to explore attractiveness. The brain has special machinery for recognizing faces. One front-on glance and a human shape among masses of others becomes a long-lost friend, a beloved family member, or an irritating coworker.

Face recognition may be "the most fine-tuned system we have," says Alice O'Toole of the University of Texas at Dallas. "However we code them neurally, we are able to keep track of what makes individual faces unique. When I look at you, I would code what makes you different from every other face I have ever seen."

Some work suggests that attractiveness is processed as a variation from the mean (which could hint at why averageness matters). In a 2007 study published in *Neuropsychologia*, participants underwent fMRI [functional magnetic resonance imaging] while viewing faces of varying degrees of attractiveness. The study suggested that people's brains have strong responses in the right amygdala—part of the brain that has been linked to both positive and negative emotions—to pretty faces and ugly faces, and less response to middle-of-the-road faces. (So ugly faces are also intense like chocolate, not because they create longing, perhaps, but fear.)

Joel Winston of University College London, an author of the study, says early brain-scanning research took a linear approach to attractiveness, finding that some brain regions responded more to attractive faces and others to unattractive faces. But the recent study included faces that fell between the extremes and found that some brain responses are elicited by unattractive and attractive faces but not less distinct faces.

Getting to the Source of Attraction

In this respect, Gangestad says, you could think of characteristics like averageness in terms of preference and avoidance. "It may well be that in our ancestral past certain kinds of mutations caused malformations of all sorts of bodily features, including the face, and that is part of what you are picking up on," he says.

Winston says the imaging studies don't look at nitty-gritty brain activity, but still hold promise. "There is some evidence in basic visual science research that with an fMRI scanner we can actually decode what the subject is looking at better than the subject can," he says. "Certainly the brain knows more about the world than you do in the sense of your conscious self."

Steve Platek of the University of Liverpool in England agrees that indicators of potential fitness ought to activate sensors in the brain. "The average person you pass on the street is probably not 'hot or not,'" he says. "But if they are hot or not, they should activate some kind of socially behavioral response [the reward circuitry] that says go after that person at all costs or avoid them at all costs because mating could be really horrific for your [offspring's] genes."

Such a drive might underlie the utility of attractiveness. And elucidating how the brain responds to large, obvious differences in attractiveness could help researchers understand how the brain responds to differences that are subconscious and difficult to articulate. Platek says he does have results, as yet unpublished, that look at the brain's response to good-gene indicators.

While computers have enabled the isolation of facial features for study, Lie says the next step will be in reassembling attractiveness—joining studies on facial features with predicted fitness and brain scans. "I have a feeling when we perceive attractiveness in the real world, it is a holistic process," she says. "It becomes more than the sum of its parts."

The next time a face catches your eye, you may not be able to articulate what turns your head or makes your heart jump, but you will certainly know what you feel. Call it instinct, call it evolution, call it what you want. It may take researchers many more years to understand why you find a super-fine face to be so sweet. But that shouldn't stop you from looking.

> "Attractiveness underlies cultural differ-
> ences as well as differentiating opinions
> over the history of mankind."

The Standards of Beauty Are Based on Culture

Lea Höfel

In the following viewpoint, Lea Höfel claims that standards of female beauty differ across cultures, civilizations, and periods in history. For instance, she writes that the ample-figured "Venus of Willendorf," a fertility statue from the Stone Age, idealizes a body built for survival during scarcity, contrasting the notions of gentleness and slimness that would follow thousands of years later. And while childlike female faces—characterized by large eyes, a small nose, and full lips—are found attractive in many parts of the world today, Höfel maintains that poorer populations and those removed from Western influence do not find thin bodies as desirable. The author is a scientist at the Institute of Psychology I at the University of Leipzig, Germany.

As you read, consider the following questions:

1. According to Höfel, what are the advantages of extreme ornamental features in wildlife?

Lea Höfel, "Beauty Under the Magnifying Glass: Is There a Universal Beauty Ideal? (Part III of 'The Psychology of Aesthetic')," *Dental Tribune*, vol. 1, 2005, pp. 16–17. Reproduced by permission.

2. How does the author describe the beauty ideal of the Middle Ages?

3. How do the Hadza of Tanzania perceive heavy women, as stated by Höfel?

Mankind has always been interested in beauty and attractiveness. The search for a universal beauty ideal is a major topic in everyday life as well as in science. Evolutionary and cognitive theories try to give answers to the question of what is perceived as being beautiful and why this is so. In social psychology, it is furthermore investigated which effects in social life correlate with an attractive appearance. . . .

All the different angles clutch at straws when deviations from the prevalent beauty ideal can be found. Attractiveness underlies cultural differences as well as differentiating opinions over the history of mankind. The main focus of this article is these differences. To exemplify this, we will create [a] fictive person that we will call Chamelea. As the name indicates, Chamelea is a very changeable person who can, depending on the time and culture we put her into, adapt her outer appearance to be considered beautiful. But before we start the time travel, we'll have a look at the evolutionary perspective of mate selection.

Evolutionary Theories

In his fundamental work *The Origin of Species*, [naturalist Charles] Darwin developed several basic principles of evolutionary selection. He argued that those beings survived who adapted to changes in the environment (natural selection). Later, he introduced the concept of sexual selection. This concept says that members of one sex seek access to the opposite sex. To achieve this, they have to compete against concurrence of their competitors (intrasexual selection). Additionally, members of the other sex are preferred if they have favorable characteristics (intersexual selection). This perspective leads to an evolutionary theory of human mate selection.

The aim of selection processes is mainly the stabilization of the species where extreme characteristics are avoided. Individuals who come closer to the population mean are less endangered of mutation than those individuals whose characteristics differentiate from the norm. Since norm-oriented individuals father descendants that also possess these stabilizing characteristics, they are preferred as potential partners and have the best selection chances.

Furthermore, sexual selection also depends on reproduction ability. Individuals who father more descendants have higher chances of survival than individuals who live longer. Following this hypothesis, on the one hand it is important to be relatively on average. On the other hand, it is advantageous to have characteristics that are different from the rest of the group in order to be noticed. This dilemma is part of [researcher Amotz Zahavi's] theory of the "sexual selection of the good genes," or the "handicap theory." Extreme ornaments like a peacock's tail feathers or a deer's antlers reduce the possibility of survival since they need enormous energy to develop and maintain them. To allow oneself the luxury of these conspicuous features the individual has to have resources in plentiful supply. Intrasexually, the ornaments help to scare the competitors. Intersexually, one will be recognized earlier than average individuals. The ornamented individual shows that he or she is strong enough to be able to develop unnecessary decoration. Despite this handicap, the animal or person can survive. Following this thought, it is sensible to differentiate from the population's mean. These differences are considered beautiful. The average face is more attractive than individual faces. But they are even more attractive if some features (e.g., large eyes) are exaggerated.

The Attraction to Immunity and Evolved Features

The connection between immunity and ornaments was investigated by [researchers W.D.] Hamilton and [M.] Zuk. The tail feathers of swallows were larger and more symmetric the more the swallow was plagued by parasites and infections. Thus, beauty is also an indication of the fact that one can fight against all adversities. The tail feathers of the swallow or the peacock are an outward sign of the birds' resistance against parasites. The greater the strain, the greater the visible triumph. A potential partner hopes to give these good immunity genes to their descendants.

All evolutionary attractiveness theories are based on the idea of the "survival of the fittest." Those partners that are in little danger of mutation and whose outward signs are linked to a high fitness level are considered beautiful.

In order to show that science is in line with everyday phenomena as well, a study by [researcher A.M.] Magro is worth noting.

Magro sees a somewhat unusual connection between evolution and the beauty ideal. On the basis of human history, he explains why Barbie is perceived as beautiful. Students evaluated drawings and photographs of persons with primitive or derived anatomical features. Ancient human beings possessed shorter legs, curved toes, a shorter neck and a broader waist than today. Students looked at two pictures that differed slightly in a single anatomical trait, but were similar in all other aspects. Results showed that the derived features were preferred. Magro then compared these derived characteristics to the Barbie doll, which was first marketed in 1959. Numerous features of the doll are comparable to human changes that have been made over the last 3 to 4 million years.

Following Magro's thoughts, Barbie reflects the prototype of human evolution. She is tall, has long legs, a narrow waist, full red lips, huge eyes, straight symmetric teeth and long fin-

Bizarre Beauty Routines

To the Kayan tribe in Burma, beauty is an elongated neck. Ethiopian women find beauty in scarring their body, whilst Polynesians acquire it through tattooing. Though some of these practices may appear excessive, they are not so different from spending hundreds of dollars on beauty products, hair extensions, . . . and tanning. Imagine how bizarre our beauty routines would appear to other cultures.

Devon Butler,
"Society Needs to Widen Its Concept of Beauty,"
CordWeekly.com, March 11, 2009.

gers, just to name a few of her derived features. Other dolls like the "Happy to Be Me" doll, for example, do not show these extreme modern features and they are by far not as popular as Barbie. Barbie shows us how we would like to be and points out the evolutionary developed anatomical features.

Even if attractiveness theories seem to be generally accepted, one should keep in mind that there is nothing like an everlasting, unique beauty ideal. Deviations and changes will be the focus of the following sections. Since men pay more attention to the appearance of women than women do to the appearance of men, most studies deal with female beauty. Due to this, female attractiveness will be the prime example.

Beauty Ideal Changes

Today's ideal is that of a rather slim woman with an hourglass figure, but this has not always been so. One can observe that in times when food was scarce and rather a luxury, rounded figures were preferred. Each epoch has its own conception of a beautiful woman. First of all, our main character Chamelea will travel back to the Stone Age. During this time period her figure can be described as having thick legs, sumptuous breasts, a round belly and huge hips. The "Venus of Willendorf" was constructed 27,000 years ago and was the fertility goddess of Stone Age people. The distribution of gynoidal fat is similar for all European fertility goddesses of that time. The fat reserves around the hip helped the mother and her children to survive in rather meager times. Additionally, these reserves were a protection against the cold.

Chamelea in old Egypt worries about her outer appearance a lot. Her eyes are highlighted with green or black colors and like her model, Cleopatra, she takes a bath in donkey or mare milk. A beautiful Egyptian woman has large eyes, a small nose, full lips and a long, slim neck. Many ancient recipes for skin and hair care are still common knowledge today in Egypt.

While the Egyptian Chamelea still has olive-colored skin, she finds herself becoming rather pale in Greek antiquity. "Whiter than ivory" is the perfect female skin for [ancient poet] Homer. Striving for aesthetic perfection led to the ideal of balanced, harmonic proportions. Marble statues such as Aphrodite, the goddess of love, which can be seen at the Louvre in Paris, are far from the ideal of Stone Age people. During Greek antiquity, people were fasting, doing sports, and went to the baths on a regular basis. Good proportions were deemed an outward sign of a good, healthy lifestyle.

Chamelea is still kind of pale in the Middle Ages. Makeup was considered heathen, so she must do without it. She has a high forehead, narrow and plucked eyebrows, a rather small mouth and a long neck. Her shoulders are small, she stands straight and pushes her belly slightly forward. Like this, she appears gentle and demure. Paintings or sculptures of that time usually show women fully dressed.

During the Renaissance, antique beauty ideals were partly rediscovered. Youthful slim figures with sloping shoulders, small breasts and a noticeable belly turn Chamelea into a beautiful woman through the 15th and 16th centuries. She is light skinned and has long blond hair that falls over her shoulders.

She seems rather sumptuous in the Baroque style. [Seventeenth-century painter Peter Paul] Rubens' drawings of plumper forms indicate that the female flesh has to be "firm, stout and white." These curves represent fertility, joy and pleasure.

Approaching the Modern Ideal

Sissi, the Empress of Austria, symbolized the ideal of the 19th century. With long black hair, pale skin, and a narrow waist, she represented the trend of that time. The dresses were very costly and, despite health risks, women wore tight corsets. This is why Chamelea happily leaves the role of the prettiest woman to Sissi and continues to travel to the 20th century. In the 1920s, emancipation begins and short haircuts are now the modern style. This changes with the Second World War. Full-figured bodies are preferred, like the hourglass figures of Marilyn Monroe and Sophia Loren, with longish flowing hair representing the ideal type of woman.

Later though, Chamelea has to go on a strict diet because slender women with huge eyes are perceived as beautiful. Models, such as Twiggy in 1966, with childlike, boyish charisma were considered to fit the modern ideal of beauty. During the '80s, the beauty ideal required a sportive and somewhat muscular figure. Keeping fit, often by aerobics, was a part of everyday life from this time forward and today's beauty ideal is often attained with the help of computer animation (Lara Croft in the video game "Tomb Raider") or body doubles (for example, Julia Roberts's legs in "Pretty Woman"). And, if there is no way to reach the preferred look naturally, plastic surgery is now also a viable option.

Considering the passage of time, it is interesting to note if older people still prefer outward signs of youth and health. From an evolutionary point of view it is possible that these fertility predictors are not that important anymore. [Researcher Devendra] Singh asked men between the ages of 25 and 85 to evaluate female figures. Results showed that men of each age group found slim, normal-weighted women attractive. There was a difference concerning underweight women though. Among the young men, 25 percent of them found these women attractive, whereas only 5 percent of the older men were of that opinion.

Furthermore, older participants did not make the associations "underweight" and "healthy." Taken together, one can state that the evaluation of attractiveness stays relatively stable over the human life span. Implicit attributions such as "healthy," "desirable" and "able to raise children" are not that strongly connected with outer appearance. It is not yet clear whether the sexual interest in a potential partner decreases or if life experience is more important for the judgment of a person, and whether such things lead to different judgment strategies. It will be interesting to see which body form Chamelea will have in the future or when she is old.

Intercultural Differences

Many studies support the opinion that there is only one universal beauty ideal that exists and is independent of cultural background. Studies from [researcher D.] Jones, for example, postulate that neotonous features, such as a childlike face with a small nose, huge eyes and full lips, are preferred by Americans in the US, people from Brazil, Russia, and Indians in Venezuela and Paraguay. [Researchers A.] Furnham, [A.] McClelland and [L.] Omer came to the conclusion that people from Kenya and Britain perceive the same female figure as attractive.

Deviations from this result were found by [researchers F.] Marlowe and [A.] Wetsman. They conducted an experiment in a hunter-gatherer society whose members were not touched by Western civilization. They asked Hadza who live in Tanzania to rank the drawings of women that had already been used as stimulus material in previous studies. The figures varied in weight (underweight, normal, overweight) and waist-to-hip ratio (WHR), from 0.7 to 0.9. In Western cultures, a normal body weight with a WHR of 0.7 is usually preferred. Contrary to these results, the Hadza found heavy women more attractive than normal women, and thought that underweight women looked rather sick. So Chamelea as a Hadza woman would have to gain weight and her WHR should be higher than 0.7.

[Researchers D.W.] Yu and [G.H.] Shepard conducted a similar experiment in Peru. They questioned Matsingenka men (Yomybato) who live in Manu Park, which is restricted to all but scientific and official visitors. There, women were judged according to their weight, with overweight women considered as being more attractive, healthy and desirable. Additionally, a population that lives outside of the park (Shietiari) but that is still not really touched by Western civilization, was also asked to judge the photos. This group also preferred overweight women and found them to be healthier. However, women with a lower WHR were judged to be more attractive and were chosen as potential mates.

The last group of men who were questioned belonged to an ethnically mixed group (Alto Madre) that lives along the Alto Madre River, which is a major trading route. Thus, these people have more contact to other populations. The results here did not differ significantly from the US population. They grouped female figures by WHR and then by weight. Taken all together, the judgments become more like those of the US population in places where it was clear that there was a stronger Western influence. Following the arguments of Marlowe and Wetsman, the WHR is of interest in those cultures that have enough food. Poorer populations and those far from Western influence look at weight as an indicator of fertility. In these populations, the danger of starvation is greater, thus a well-fed woman is more desirable than a skinny one.

> "If a preference for mixed-race faces oc-
> curs for many different mixes, we could
> be more confident that it is tapping into
> something fundamental about human
> perceptions of attractiveness."

The Standards of Beauty Are Becoming Multiracial

William Lee Adams

In the following viewpoint, William Lee Adams proposes that the exotic looks of mixed-raced people are changing the perception of beauty. For instance, Adams claims that models who are half-Asian and half-Caucasian, or "hapa" in Hawaiian slang, now dominate fashion runways in Asia. Furthermore, he states that a study reveals that both Japanese and Caucasian subjects rated Eurasian faces the most attractive and healthiest looking, even among faces of their own races. A possible explanation, Adams concludes, for the appeal of multiracial beauty is genetic diversity, which is associated with lower incidence of genetic disease. Adams reports for the London bureau of Time *magazine.*

William Lee Adams, "Mixed Race, Pretty Face? Why We're Drawn to Exotic Beauty," *Psychology Today*, vol. 39, January-February 2006, pp. 17–8. Copyright © 2006 Sussex Publishers, Inc. LLC. Reproduced by permission.

As you read, consider the following questions:

1. Not including mixed races, what characterized subjects' responses about ideals of beauty in the study the author cites?

2. As stated by the author, what can happen to infants exposed to toxins or pathogens in the womb?

3. In Adams's view, what mating theory does the preference for mixed-race faces counter?

Actor Keanu Reeves and supermodel Devon Aoki have more in common than fame, fortune and good looks—both are also part Asian. Known in popular culture by the Hawaiian term "hapa" (meaning "half"), people with mixed Asian and European origins have become synonymous with exotic glamour. In Hong Kong and Singapore, half-Asian models now crowd runways once dominated by leggy blondes. In the elite world of Asian fashion, half-Asian is the new white.

The trend may seem little more than an effect of 21st century globalization. As more individuals of mixed descent achieve fame (think [singer] Norah Jones and [golfer] Tiger Woods), it seems natural that society would embrace the mixed look. Media exposure, however, doesn't fully explain the perception of hapa beauty.

Eurasians may possess genetic advantages that lead to greater health and, as a result, enhanced attractiveness. That's according to a study, the first to find that hapa faces are rated as more beautiful than European or Japanese faces. Researchers say the finding may extend to other racial mixes as well. The experiment by Gillian Rhodes, a psychologist at the University of Western Australia, found that when Caucasian and Japanese volunteers looked at photos of Caucasian, Japanese, and Eurasian faces, both groups rated the Eurasian faces as most attractive. These visages were created by first digitally blending a series of faces from each race into "composites" to

Racial Purity Is Biological Nonsense

The idea of racial purity as the highest form of perfection was taken to its extreme by Adolf Hitler, whose warped beliefs led to the death of six million Jews. [British psychology expert George] Fieldman said: "Inbreeding is not great news. All that bollocks about blue blood is just nonsense. The Nazis were terrible scientists. At a biological level it was just nonsense."

Steve Bloomfield,
"The Face of the Future: Why Eurasians Are Changing the
Rules of Attraction," Independent (UK), *January 15, 2006.*

create average, middle-of-the-road features typical of each race. Past studies show that "average" features are consistently rated as more attractive than exaggerated features—such as an unusually wide forehead or a small chin.

The finding that Japanese and white subjects preferred mixed-race faces was surprising because, earlier in the same study, most volunteers rated their own race as more beautiful than others. That is, white people typically prefer whites when choosing an ideal image of beauty; blacks prefer blacks; etc.

Genetic Diversity Is Attractive

So why might hapas be considered particularly beautiful? Evolutionary psychologists say it's because Eurasians and other mixed-race individuals appear healthier. Humans, like other animals, look for markers of good genetic health in their quest for a reproductive partner. Take facial symmetry, for example: Studies show that, whether they know it or not, people prefer individuals with evenly spaced eyes and other signs of congruence. In evolutionary terms, these markers are associated with healthy conditions in the womb. Infants exposed prenatally to toxins or pathogens may develop facial irregularities and asymmetry. The human brain may be wired to avoid these overt cues of lackluster health, says R. Elisabeth Cornwell, a psychologist at the University of Colorado. "The signs of beauty are the signs of health," she says. Rhodes' findings seem to fit this paradigm: Participants in her study said the Eurasian faces appeared healthier, too.

Similarly, evidence suggests that half-Asians' diverse genetic ancestry would enhance health. According to evolutionary psychologist Randy Thornhill, at the University of New Mexico, "If you hybridize two genetically diverse populations—another way of saying you cross races—then you create more genetic diversity in the offspring."

Genetic diversity, or heterozygosity, is associated with a lower incidence of some diseases. Genetic diseases, such as hemophilia and Tay-Sachs, occur when a person inherits two copies of a defective gene. This is more likely to happen in isolated populations with little genetic diversity.

Last year [in 2005], Craig Roberts, professor of biology at the University of Newcastle in the U.K., found the first direct link between diverse genes and facial attractiveness. He examined genes of the major histocompatability complex (MHC)—a set of genes crucial to a well-functioning immune system. Photos of people with the greatest MHC diversity were rated more attractive than individuals with less MHC diversity. Here, actual health—the ability to resist infection—was linked to perceptions of attractiveness. Roberts believes this preference helps humans pick healthy mates.

Which features radiate both health and beauty? One may be the appearance of the skin. In a second experiment, Roberts found that women rated close-up photos of heterozygous males' skin as healthier than close-ups of homozygous males' skin, and these judgments correlated with ratings of overall attractiveness.

Ostensibly, evidence that Caucasians and Asians prefer mixed-race faces counters a major tenet of mating theory: that we are drawn to partners who resemble ourselves, such as those with similar hair and eye color.

So does this new research explain the popularity of Brazilians, who frequently have blended racial heritage, as fashion models? That remains to be seen. Says Rhodes: "If a preference for mixed-race faces occurs for many different mixes, we could be more confident that it is tapping into something fundamental about human perceptions of attractiveness."

> "As definitions of beauty become ever more exacting, and as the shape-shifting technology required to maintain that aesthetic carries on developing, a homogenisation of faces is taking place."

The Standards of Beauty Are Homogenous

Joanna Briscoe

Joanna Briscoe is a British author. She has contributed to publications such as the Guardian, *the* Independent, *and* Vogue. *In the following viewpoint, Briscoe contends that the rigid beauty standards amplified in the media are trickling down to the masses as physical ideals. Briscoe states that, because their looks are their livelihood, actors, models, and other celebrities are going blond as a prerequisite for fame and conforming to unnatural requirements of youthfulness and thinness—often under the scalpel of the same cosmetic surgeon. In turn, the definition of beauty in Hollywood and beyond is increasingly homogenized, and perceptions of a normal or desirable human body are altered, says the author.*

Joanna Briscoe, "Haven't I Seen You Somewhere?" *Guardian*, January 17, 2004. Reproduced by permission of Guardian News Service, LTD.

As you read, consider the following questions:

1. How does Briscoe describe the current beauty ideal?

2. How has rhinoplasty changed in Hollywood throughout the decades, as stated by the author?

3. In the author's view, why is the public accountable for reinforcing unrealistic cultural beauty standards?

The face was once finite, a unique set of features and a mirror of the soul. You were born with it, lived with it, aged with it, and died with it. Now it's a movable feast: a playground and a battlefield where skin, flesh, and bone are manipulated and the cultural and aesthetic standards of an era are stamped. As definitions of beauty become ever more exacting, and as the shape-shifting technology required to maintain that aesthetic carries on developing, a homogenisation of faces is taking place. In the public eye, especially, people are beginning to look more and more alike.

Somewhere in the collective consciousness nestles a creepy, standard Ur-face, a faint paradigm, subliminally recognisable as the look of our time. It comprises an inflated upper lip, precise eyebrows, perfectly aligned white teeth, and toned planes of flesh, the accompanying body usually exceptionally thin but for improbably large breasts. Somehow, what we expect to see on women of all ages conforms to those standards, from Courteney Cox Arquette to Liz Hurley, from Gisele Bundchen to Melanie Griffith, Shirley MacLaine to Catherine Deneuve, while the more natural-featured sexagenarian Brigitte Bardot appears, in contrast, as something of a shock. In failing to conform fully to the unnatural standard, Bardot is perceived to have "let herself go," her looks little short of an aesthetic affront.

The Celebrity Influence

Meanwhile, in the shadows, a male equivalent is subtly evolving. As fluently as we can evoke the simian encyclopedia-drawn features of Piltdown man, we can summon a portrait of Movie man. He starts off as Heath Ledger or Orlando Bloom, buffs up to become Brad Pitt or Tom Cruise, and gradually morphs into Martin Sheen, Michael Douglas, Arnold Schwarzenegger, or Julio Iglesias, all taut, puppety jawline, dead eyes, and bronze lowlights. Many of the movers and shakers whose images inform our daily lives appear distantly related.

Such uniformity is nothing new. The arched eyebrows, regimented waves, and crimson-painted slab of a mouth once favoured by Joan Crawford, Marlene Dietrich, and their contemporaries, supplemented by the rudimentary tug-and-stretch face-lifts of that era, added up to a certain level of homogeneity that was then echoed by the masses. By the early 1960s, Marilyn Monroe had had her chin implant, and the scalpel began to play a vital role in the Hollywood star system. But now that cosmetic procedures—from skin peels and collagen injections to lower-body lifts—are almost obligatory for those in the entertainment industry, people can resemble each other at a far more profound level, at the level of their actual features, and therefore their expressions and general demeanour.

People simply look less like themselves. The actor Meg Ryan, whose normal lips had previously sufficed, recently adopted a "trout pout" that made her momentarily unrecognisable, bearing more of a resemblance to [actor] Leslie Ash and Melanie Griffith than her previous self. The Melanie Griffith, that is, whose shapeless cushion of a mouth is lodged uncomfortably beneath her girlish nose and pulled-taut eyes, and who, in turn, bears a fleeting surgical resemblance to Courtney Love. The older these people become, the more they mutate to resemble one another, so that the tribes of pensionable social x-rays that people *Hello!* look uncannily alike, while Kirk and Michael Douglas appear to be standing in the same wind tunnel, with Charlton Heston a few paces further along.

The Loss of Aesthetic Diversity

Homogenisation is happening at an earlier stage, too. In this era of manufactured pop, singers are preselected so that they all look similar in the first place. With fewer organically formed groups, the rogue looks factor is diminished: there is now far less chance of a Pogue tooth or a Streisand nose slipping on to Top of the Pops. (The recent *Pop Idol* winner may have momentarily bucked the trend, but even so, much press attention remains focused on her looks.)

The proliferation of celebrity means that even reality TV C-listers, who give a misleading impression of "normality," have been selected, styled, and then digitally enhanced, spreading a diluted solution of the same aesthetic. The remoulding of one's own body is a more effective path to contemporary celebrity than the honing of any questionable talent.

But why do celebrities—and, by a trickle-down process, the rest of us—crave an approximation of the same image? At its simplest, as Desmond Morris, zoologist and author of *People Watching*, says, "Nowadays, they do all want to look alike because they can."

The Barbie prototype has taken a firm hold, but the reasons for its desirability are rarely questioned. "It's a composite of idealised features that are connected to cultural fantasies," says Virginia L. Blum, author of *Flesh Wounds: The Culture of Cosmetic Surgery*. "A lot of these are comic-book features, and that emphasises the plasticity of the body—comic books were always a parody of, for example, the wasp waist, but now the real body can exaggerate the measurements considered desirable, based on the image world."

Planet of the Blondes

Blondes have taken over at a time when a team of German scientists has predicted that authentic adult blondes, those scarce pale oddities, will die out within the next two centuries, since too few people carry the blond gene. It makes perverse sense. As with all scarce commodities, rarity is inevitably valued, so even though any cash-strapped adolescent can hit the peroxide, the resulting colour, however bogus, is still indicative of some kind of exclusivity. Blondes have been simultaneously perceived as symbols of comforting stupidity, purity, and sexual availability for a couple of millennia. The myth began, according to Joanna Pitman, author of *On Blondes,* in the fourth century BC, when the hair of Praxiteles's Aphrodite of Cnidus was tinted gold. During the past century at least, blondness has, more worryingly, been associated with racial purity, with a white and potentially fair-haired elite, economically superior to darker and less powerful ethnic groups.

Blondness, as in "baby blond," is perennially equated with precious youth, since natural blondness frequently fades post-toddlerhood, and the magnified, numinous glow of golden-haired nubility has become a silver-screen standard. "Blondes are the best victims," said Alfred Hitchcock. "They're like virgin snow which shows up the bloody footprints."

Hollywood was always the planet of the blondes, though brunettes were far more dominant in the 30s and 40s than they are now, but add to the current A-list firmament a sizeable majority of soap actors, TV presenters, VJs [video performance artists], models, pop stars, footballers' wives and amorphous socialites, and it's apparent that blondness is both the contemporary default mode and a prerequisite of instant celebrity. The term "non-blond" has entered the language, and brunette exceptions such as Catherine Zeta-Jones are automatically tagged "exotic."

Thinness, as we know, has reached extremes—the arguments have raged for decades, yet malnourishment is still a catwalk requirement. The average model, dancer, and actor is calculated to be thinner than 95% of the population; the reduction in breast size that inevitably goes with such skinniness is alleviated by the implantation of false breasts at a cost of several thousand pounds per operation, feeding both the beauty and dieting industries.

In a Surgical Age

Evolutionary psychologists claim there is an underlying standard script for beauty—a foundation for what we find appealing that transcends culture and ethnicity. There are various absolutes. For instance, to judge someone beautiful, the eye requires symmetry. There is a principle called the Divine Proportion, or Golden Section, which was outlined by Euclid in 300 BC and which describes a set of measurements that we unconsciously find pleasing. If you look at the human face, body, a classic painting, or, for instance, a butterfly's wing or fir cone, and measure distances between various points, they will repeatedly conform to a certain fixed ratio. In people considered beautiful, they conform more precisely: if a gauge that measures the Golden Section is placed against a model's face, the distances between features usually correlate exactly.

But now that faces can be broken, cut and stitched into place, implants added and teeth straightened, we have reached a point of fearful—indeed, frightful—symmetry. We live, as [author and feminist] Naomi Wolf said, in a surgical age. Individuality is engulfed by the quest for perfect proportion. The Caucasian beauty standard has spread globally, and just as operations to "westernise" oriental eyes have become increasingly popular, so the ideal has become more and more limited. Golden-haired Beyoncé Knowles and Oscar-winner Halle Berry have been annexed to the prevailing white aesthetic. (And it is, pretty much without exception, a white aesthetic that dominates the entertainment industry and cosmetic surgery business.)

Yet notions of beauty do change quite radically, so it's fairly puzzling to see photographs of [actor] Lillie Langtry, for example, who was considered a great beauty in her day, yet to us looks inexplicably heavy-featured and generally devoid of appeal. Similarly, by the middle of the 21st century, the rake-thin, otherworldly beauty of model Erin O'Connor will surely appear alien. As will the appeal of [singer] Dannii Minogue, with her wide eyes and large globes for breasts.

Different economic, social, and cultural forces conspire to mould the current aesthetic: what we might perceive as classic has always been through the wash of contemporary cultural conditioning. For example, it's not hard to date nose jobs (rhinoplasty). In the 40s, noses such as vaudeville star Fanny Brice's were "bobbed," ridding their wearers of all ethnicity and gravity. The original *Forsyte Saga* actor Susan Hampshire, who admits to rhinoplasty, appears to sport the tip-tilted version of the late 60s, when ideal noses were small and girlish, whereas by the 80s and 90s nose jobs were designed along stronger, straighter lines, as exemplified by that of the actor Natasha Richardson.

The homogenisation of beauty creates a tribal identity—and simultaneous lack of identity—as surely as the more obvious practices of scarification and piercing, but at some level the eye isn't fooled. "It would seem we do have an intrinsic natural apprehension of the artifice that goes into creating the illusion of beauty," says the clinical psychologist Oliver James. Nature simply doesn't produce a cheese-sliced nose tapering from width at the brow to a narrower point, nor a glossy, wife-battered blur of a mouth, nor child-wide eyes in the middle-aged. But the more rigorously our vision is trained to appreciate the artificial, the more a multitude of industries benefits.

Perceptions Have Been Altered

The current standard of beauty feeds the fashion, beauty, diet, surgery, entertainment, media, and pornography industries, just for starters, the homogenisation of appearance having become part and parcel of an increasingly globalised consumer culture. Like children who are marketed certain toys before the Christmas frenzy, we have to be flogged a limited range of desirable options, one that doesn't permit us to develop an idiosyncratic and disastrous desire for the equivalent of rag dolls and sticks rather than Beyblades and Barbies. Wherever would several highly lucrative industries be if we started favouring ballooning curves, mousy hair, whiteheads, and bulbous noses? "The link to consumer culture means that the stakes have to be raised to keep us panting, our hopes unfulfilled," says Blum.

Such a rigid aesthetic subtly alters our perceptions of what's normal or desirable. "You hardly see anyone who looks her age or his age on television anymore," says Kathy Davis, author of *Reshaping the Female Body*. "I remember watching a movie and seeing a young actress who had a slightly hanging breast, and thinking, 'Oh, what's wrong with her breast?' Which shows how your perception is changed by surgery—you're just not used to seeing normal breasts."

Perception is altered, and then a new prototype develops to become an acquired taste. Thus Victoria Beckham, who has become an otherworldly creature—a twig with torpedo breasts, a lip-glossed lollipop—would appear like a highly polished anomaly in the Tesco [grocery] car park, but looks halfway normal, or even covetable, in *Heat* magazine.

[British-known celebrities] Caprice, Patsy Kensit, Jordan, and, indeed, Dannii Minogue are fascinating as a spectacle to other women and give off the raciest of subtexts to men: if a woman is prepared to suffer considerable pain to be remoulded to male specifications, what is she prepared to do in bed? The message also soothingly restores gender imbalance to compensate for success: she may earn millions, but she's no ballbreaking Amazon—she even cut herself up to look like Barbie. As Davis says, "I'm wondering whether, as women become more emancipated, it's appealing to see these young, helpless, wide-eyed innocent women—or very sick, emaciated women. It alleviates certain anxieties. Because women are get-

The Ordinarily Beautiful

There's an extraordinary high concentration of gorgeous females in Los Angeles, and courtesy of the usually balmy weather and lifestyle, they tend to be highly visible—and not just locally. The film and television industries project their images all over the world, not to mention all the supporting media dealing with celebrities and gossip that help keep them professionally viable.

As the head of a public relations agency, I work with these women day and night. You might expect that to make me feel good, as we normally like being around attractive people. But my exposure to extreme beauty is ruining my capacity to love the ordinarily beautiful women of the real world, who are more likely to meet my needs for deep connection and partnership of the soul.

Michael Levine and Hara Estroff Marano,
"Why I Hate Beauty," Psychology Today, *July-August 2001.*

ting scary." In 2000, 89% of cosmetic procedures in the US were carried out on women and 85% of surgeons were men. In the UK, it's estimated that 90% of patients are women.

Not all facial standardisation is intentional: it also occurs inadvertently as a result of wanting to look younger. Actresses face almost insurmountable pressures. "We have to remember it's their livelihood," says Blum. "The problem with actresses is that we extend all this imaginary power to them because they're these iconic images, but in real life they're the low end of the production machinery. Their careers are absolutely over if they don't do something."

Limited Aesthetic Options

The surgical palette is quite limited, so advanced technology in fact limits aesthetic options more rigidly than make-up or hair dye. "You don't have people going in saying, 'I want a really big Italian nose,'" says Elizabeth Haiken, author of *Venus Envy*. "A Hollywood surgeon is going to make all his star patients look alike," says Blum, "because that's the look he likes, and he uses the same kind of techniques. The patients all start out different and they converge."

Surgery also inadvertently blurs the signs of gender, those unruffled, taut surfaces and retracted hairlines masculinising older women, just as the smooth skin created by face-lifting, blepharoplasty (eyelid lifting), and microdermabrasion results in a faintly feminine look in men. Even hair dye can feminise. Aubergine-locked Paul McCartney suddenly bears a faint resemblance to a chubby-cheeked, middle-aged woman of the Angela Lansbury variety, with [European singers] Cilla Black and Lulu somewhere on the continuum, while a tribe of ageing public figures—Nancy Reagan, Joan Rivers, Barbara Walters, Lily Safra, Helen Gurley Brown, and Mary Tyler Moore—shows a collective resemblance as the surgically created impression of immobile androgyny progresses.

But why such an extreme aversion to age? Again, the rare and unattainable is prized. Western society is by and large a mouse-to-brunette-to-grey ageing population with a growing obesity problem. The young, thin blonde, amplified and godlike on screen, is therefore the ideal. As a society, our mental and emotional perceptions lag behind our own unprecedented longevity—we simply cannot face the unpleasant consequences of extreme old age, and nothing in our culture has so far prepared us for them. The signs of ageing are perceived as so repellent that many in the public eye actively choose a deeply strange and clearly artificial appearance over a reflection of their actual years. In a world of quasi-clones, the alien is normal: "There are all these older actresses who have become unrecognisable," says Blum. "But this is a subculture where it's perfectly OK to look surgical. They're among their peer group, and they all look the same."

"We've evolved from small tribes, where we would follow the tribal dictates," says Desmond Morris. "Now every young girl wants to be Britney Spears or Beyoncé Knowles—they don't want to look like the girl at No17 anymore because these are the tribal templates, and so you get homogenisation and you have blond hair streaking and people trying to look like Britney in Japan."

"In cultures that emphasise the importance of appearance," says Blum, "when you notice that you don't look a certain way—you don't have your eyebrows waxed or you're not as blond as you should be—first of all, people feel shame. The second stage is that they identify with the thing they should be and try to become it. For celebrities, it's like watching their shame on the big screen. They aren't outside of this machinery—they are at its centre. They feel the same inadequacy that the rest of us feel, but in relation to their own iconic images."

The standardisation, or what Haiken terms "the medicalisation of appearance," doesn't stop with features. Expressions follow suit, because Oscar-winning emoting is pretty hard to pull off with nerve damage and muscle paralysis. Last year [in 2003], producers and directors, seemingly oblivious to the fact that their industry has played a major part in setting such draconian aesthetic standards, began to bewail the fact that facial surgery and the "pretty poison" botox were limiting actors' expressions. Casting director Paul de Freitas was quoted as saying, "We're forever getting actresses who have had so much botox that they simply can't move their faces anymore."

Who Creates the Culture?

According to the American Society for Aesthetic Plastic Surgery, the number of cosmetic procedures in the US more than doubled between 1997 and 2002. Overall, botox treatments have increased 16-fold in the past four years, while clinical trials found that 40% of those procedures caused some adverse side effects. It seems fitting that a beauty product that could double up as a weapon of mass destruction is viewed as little more than a form of make-up in the film industry. So, yes, actors are somewhat hindered when it comes to wielding the full range of thespian skills, but this is a case in point: the culture and the industries behind it should be blamed, rather than the reconfigured bit-players who respond with varying degrees of willingness. "It's better to think of the culture as pathological as opposed to the individual," says Davis.

But who creates that culture? However much we may confidently point the finger at certain industries and the predominantly male powers behind them, we can't deny our own tacit, albeit culturally conditioned, involvement. The celebrity phenomenon undoubtedly works two ways. However emphatically we may scorn the excessive eyebrow threading, facial surgery, Ashtanga yoga, and airbrushing that lies behind the polished image, we still require the silver screen's vastly magnified faces to be easy on the eye. It's like organic fruit. We all think we desire pesticide-free nuggets of earthy goodness, but we're revolted by the accompanying mouldy knobbles and insect life. We want to aspire, ogle, imitate, and we want tales of romantic incompetence and botched botox—just not at the same time. The biggest-selling issues of celebrity magazines such as *Heat* might be the ones with the cruellest off-duty snaps (cellulite, sweat stains, bad bikinis), but we really don't want to see open pores and eye bags on MTV or at the cinema. And so the skin is resurfaced, the eye bags excised, and our celluloid heroes slowly and inexorably converge.

As M.G. Lord wrote in *Forever Barbie*, "The postsurgical Dolly Parton looks like the postsurgical Ivana Trump looks like the postsurgical Michael Jackson looks like the postsurgical Joan Rivers looks like . . . Barbie."

It's no coincidence that *The Stepford Wives* [film] is being remade. Whether or not we like it, carving knives and poisons and bovine solutions are the woad and lead oxide of our times, and a strange clan of replicants of the anorexic, trout-pouting, albino variety has become as visible to us on a daily basis as our neighbours. Beauty is no longer truth.

"*Increasingly, physical perfection is a bonus, not a necessity, in America's benchmark of beauty.*"

The Standards of Beauty Are Changing

Christine Lennon

The backlash against cosmetic surgery and the pursuit of conventional beauty has begun, writes Christine Lennon in the following viewpoint, and notions of beauty are becoming more diverse in the media. She states that reality shows depicting cosmetic operations have turned off viewers and Newsweek's multiracial pick for the "perfect" face reflects broadening ideals of who is pretty. While attractiveness has a basis in genetics and evolution, Lennon claims that increasing ethnic populations and exposure to atypical faces are transforming standards of beauty in America.

As you read, consider the following questions:

1. According to the viewpoint, what has happened to the conventional "pretty face"?

Christine Lennon, "Your Changing Ideal of Pretty," *Marie Claire*, vol. 12, October 2005, pp. 130–133. Copyright 2005 © Hearst Communications, Inc. All rights reserved. Reproduced by permission.

2. How does Frank Galasso describe the girls at L.A. Models?

3. What are some traits belonging to the women who appear in the author's list of unconventional beauties?

You love Jennifer Aniston's look; you adore Sarah Jessica Parker's style. Yet neither is what your mother would call a "classic beauty." After the huge cosmetic-surges boom, has plastic perfection finally overstayed its welcome? *Marie Claire* explores how women are turning "flaws" into trademarks, creating a whole new idea of what's pretty now.

Remember when "pretty" referred to a handful of Western-looking models who were virtually interchangeable, give or take a mole? Ask women today who's pretty, and the examples vary as much as the looks they represent. The only thing they have in common is the fact that none of them are "perfect."

Natural Features Are More Often Admired

Increasingly, physical perfection is a bonus, not a necessity, in America's benchmark of beauty. One reason: As cosmetic surgery makes it possible for women to purchase "perfect" features, the mystique of what was once unattainable has diminished. "The conventional 'pretty face' used to be rare," says Teresa Riordan, author of *Inventing Beauty*. "Now, you can shop for a new face like people used to shop for makeup. It makes the traditional ideal of beauty less exciting. People start searching for something new."

Does the new definition of pretty equal natural? That seems to be the trend cosmetic surgeons are seeing. "When I started my practice, every 17-year-old girl from Long Island was getting rhinoplasty," says Z. Paul Lorenc, M.D., F.A.C.S. [Fellow of the American College of Surgeons], a New York plastic surgeon. "Sixteen years later [in 2005], it's OK not to have a perfect nose. Different is sexy." Some patients even ask to keep a small bump, says Dr. Lorenc, so their nose won't

look like the one all their friends just bought. "There's much more diversity in the appearance of our movie and music icons now," he adds. "The message is, different is good."

Reality television also factors into the turning of the tide. Watching women with low self-esteem submit to painful procedures on shows like *The Swan* makes some consumers think twice about going under the knife. "People in Los Angeles are hyper-aware of the 'plastic-surgery look'—and it's not what people want to see anymore," says Frank Galasso, a stylist and owner of L.A.'s frank.studio. "I work with L.A. Models, and all the new girls have natural-looking noses and teeth. A gap in the teeth—that's what we like now. A unique look. Reality TV made 'plastic-surgery beauty' so overexposed, we are finally seeing a backlash."

Even surgeons say TV's depiction of cosmetic operations can be a turnoff for clients. In a survey of 4,000 doctors by Castle Connolly Medical, Ltd., an independent health-care research company, nearly 40 percent said that *The Swan* had a negative impact on the public's ideas of the cosmetic-surgery industry; only 5 percent approved of the message behind MTV's *I Want a Famous Face*, in which participants undergo surgery to look like celebrities.

Viewers seem to be losing interest, too: Ratings for such reality-TV shows continue to slide. "Nobody likes perfection anymore. It's over," says trend forecaster Faith Popcorn. "Beauty is following the population, which is becoming more diverse." In 2004, *Newsweek* selected Saira Mohan, a model of Indian, French, and Irish descent, to represent "The Perfect Face" for a story about beauty ideals. "Many people see something of themselves in me," says Mohan. "Maybe that's why they call me pretty."

Who Decides What's Pretty?

1. *Doctors in labs.* Researchers have devoted entire careers to defining beauty. "The perception of facial beauty boils down to two factors: how attracted you are to someone's face, and whether it evokes a positive emotional response in you," says Stephen Marquardt, M.D., a maxillofacial reconstructive surgeon and researcher in the study of human attractiveness. Both factors can be predicted by a mathematical formula for facial symmetry, says Dr. Marquardt.

2. *Darwin.* Evolution may have programmed people's brains to identify beauty from birth. A study from the University of Exeter in England found that newborn babies are more attracted to a "beautiful" face than to an average one.

3. *Women around the world.* Research suggests that our sense of beauty is also informed by neurological "imprinting." Essentially, your brain constantly compiles images of faces it sees and averages them, forming a beauty blueprint based on those averages. The more ethnic and atypical faces you're exposed to, the broader your beauty standard becomes. (But, regardless of ethnicity, symmetrical features are always considered more desirable.) "Our brain seems to form a composite. If we've only seen white faces of Northern European descent, that's what we think is beautiful. The more we experience, the more our beauty perceptions change," says Nancy Etcoff, Ph.D., a Harvard psychologist and author of *Survival of the Prettiest: The Science of Beauty.* The diversity of today's cities—and, to a certain extent, the media we're exposed to—is having an impact on our sense of beauty, says Dr. Etcoff. "We're exposed to people from more countries than ever, especially with the U.S. population boom of Asians and Hispanics. We incorporate these features into our beauty ideals."

These women weren't pretty in the traditional sense—but their quirks endeared them to us:

- Lucille Ball: Proof that goofy redheads can be gorgeous.

- Edie Sedgwick: Jet-black eyes + short blonde hair = sexy punk-rock pioneer.

- Tina Turner: Dynamo energy meets mile-long legs—an American sex symbol was born.

- Lauren Hutton: Her famous tooth gap spawned a four-decade career.

- Katharine Hepburn: An angular face and tomboy frame made Hepburn the thinking man's—and woman's—starlet.

- Barbra Streisand: Score one for pronounced profiles: Babs refuses to alter her dramatic nose.

- Grace Jones: Some people called this '80s icon scary, but she stole the spotlight as 007's seductress in *A View to a Kill*.

Top Models, Then and Now

Today's fashion icons challenge the notion of traditional beauty:

Then: Somalia-born Iman was a trailblazing model in the '70s and '80s, but her fine features still reflected a European ideal.

Then: Christie Brinkley, reigning blonde of the '80s, had a traditional nose and delicate chin.

Then: Christy Turlington's pointy nose and puckered mouth represented a more exotic beauty in the age of the supermodels.

Now: Sudanese model Alek Wek has broader, but no less beautiful, features and a less conventional look.

Now: Blonde-of-the-moment Karolina Kurkova has a prominent nose, extra-large teeth, and narrow eyes.

Now: Current "exotic" favorite Natalia Vodianova has softer cheekbones and an unusually shaped face.

Periodical Bibliography

The following articles have been selected to supplement the diverse views presented in this chapter.

Robin Givhan
"Rounding Off Their Figures," *Washington Post,* February 16, 2007.

Glamour
"Your Race, Your Looks," February 2008.

Ronald E. Goldstein
"Can Changing Concepts of Beauty Change You?" *Season Magazine,* October 2005.

Kate Harding
"Does a Recession Change the Beauty Standard?" *Salon,* March 13, 2009.

Roger Highfield
"Symmetry Really Is Sexy Say Scientists," *Telegraph,* October, 10, 2007.

Independent
"The Secrets of Attraction: What Makes a Person Desirable?" January 16, 2008.

Sheryl McCarthy
"'Blonde Is Beautiful' Mystique," *USA Today,* January 18, 2006.

Gail Rosenblum
"Girls Strike Back at Pop Culture's Beauty Ideal," *Star Tribune,* June 5, 2008.

Claire Soares
"Women Rethink a Big Size That Is Beautiful But Brutal," *Christian Science Monitor,* July 11, 2006.

OPPOSING
VIEWPOINTS®
SERIES

CHAPTER 2

How Do Images of Beauty Affect Society?

Chapter Preface

In May 2009, Britain's Channel 4 began airing *Extreme Male Beauty*, a reality series depicting what several men are willing to do to attain physical perfection. "With chiselled flesh and perfect grooming the norm, now it's men feeling the pressure to look great," the series' Web site declares. In the first four episodes, English radio presenter Tim Shaw goes to extreme lengths to improve his appearance, from following a rigorous fitness routine to having follicles bloodily excised from the back of his head for a hair transplant. Reflecting upon his experiences on *Extreme Male Beauty*, Shaw admits, "Loads of men worry about their appearance, but they don't talk about it because it's not considered masculine. It's all a secret."[1]

With the arrival of so-called metrosexuals—heterosexual men who pay fastidious attention to how they look and what they wear—numerous commentators agree that male beauty standards are turning the table. Journalist Byron Rempel says, "Men have suffered through something women have had to endure for centuries: the idealized, air-brushed ideal of the male body, complete with almost rippling abs and a well-endowed groin area."[2] He goes on to state that guys are under increased pressure to be in shape and appear youthful, and more are turning to the gym, dieting, and cosmetic surgery. Nonetheless, Rempel insists that "the fairer sex" is still upheld to double standards physically: "What is unfortunate for women, however, is that they're still in the early stages of gaining equality with men. That means that not only do they often adopt the stress of providing and achieving, but they also have to deal with society's demands for beauty."[3] In the following chapter, the authors examine the extent to which these demands affect both sexes in their professional, social, and personal lives.

Notes

1. www.channelfour.com, April 30, 2009.
2. askmen.com, December 10, 2008.
3. askmen.com, December 10, 2008.

| "It hit Ann that these models were the pinnacle of beauty that society was holding up as every woman's ideal, yet it still was not good enough."

The Images of Beauty Are Unrealistic and Hurt Women

Kirsten Anderberg

Kirsten Anderberg is a contributor to off our backs, *which is the longest running feminist newspaper in the United States. In the following viewpoint, Anderberg alleges that the unattainable standards of female beauty that are perpetuated by the modeling and beauty industries hurt women. This emphasis on looks has led women to hate their bodies and spend countless dollars on unnecessary beauty products and weight-loss solutions, asserts Anderberg. Women are burdened by body hatred so much so that even thin women are made to feel that they need to lose weight, argues Anderberg. Women need to take back their body esteem from the beauty industry, states Anderberg, and focus on more important things, such as the economy.*

Kirsten Anderberg, "Radical Body Politics for Women," *off our backs*, November–December 2004, pp. 54–55. Reproduced by permission.

As you read, consider the following questions:

1. Who is Ann Simonton and why did she turn her attention to body activism?

2. What are some of the protests that were carried out at the Miss California Pageants in the 1980s?

3. What are some forms of simple radical body activism?

Women's Body Esteem is big business. Billions of dollars are spent on the "weight loss industry" yearly. That industry is solely dependent on women's self-hatred. Women are reduced to size, told to be less, told to shed big chunks of themselves for acceptance. Likewise, the "beauty industry" has convinced millions of women that chemical crap on their faces, and plucked eyebrows that are drawn back on, is "beauty." Additionally, the "sanitary protection industry" is here to protect society and women from supposedly toxic and shameful menstrual fluids that must be hidden and sanitized. May I suggest the very radical political action of robbing these industries of your body hatred dollars?

I first became aware of the women's body esteem movement in 1983, in Santa Cruz, California. Ann Simonton, a former cover model for *Sports Illustrated* Swimsuit Edition, *Cosmo*, CoverGirl, etc., turned her attentions to body activism shortly after a revelation in a dressing room with other models. She was getting ready for a photo shoot with other famous models and they were all complaining about different parts of their bodies. Their necks, their thighs, their stomachs, their eyes ... And it hit Ann that these models were the pinnacle of beauty that society was holding up as every woman's ideal, yet it still was not good enough. Their photos from the shoot would be airbrushed. Ann realized the modeling industry was promoting an unattainable standard of beauty for women.

Miss California Pageant Protests

In 1980, Ann joined with Nikki Craft and began to organize brilliant protests at the annual Miss California Pageants that were held nearby in Santa Cruz. These protests educated the entire region to these issues. First, ribbon-wrapped meat was thrown on stage during the bathing suit competition. Then in 1981, a very gaudy flatbed truck began to circulate the streets of Santa Cruz, with live contestants wearing banners that said "Miss Behavin'," "Miss Understood," etc., as they waved, and signs on the vehicle read "No More Profits Off Women's Bodies" and "Myth California: Never Again Uncontested." Songs such as "Thank Heaven for Little Girls" blared off the float. By the actual coronation night, about 250 protesters in costumes surrounded the Santa Cruz Civic Auditorium. The float was now full of 100 hand-made porcelain Barbie Dolls, all from the same mold, but they each had banners saying things like "Miss Chevious," and "Miss Ogyny." Some threw up at porcelain toilets. A sign that said "Is it Art or is it Politics?" adorned the float as it circled the auditorium. Three activists with tickets entered the auditorium, pulled out red lipstick and drew war paint on their faces, as they stood by the doors passing out fliers.

By the time I arrived on the scene, protesters were running one of their own, Michelle Anderson, as Miss Santa Cruz. She had become first runner up in one contest, and then won as Miss Santa Cruz in 1988. Michelle, with Ann as a coach, referred to her victories as being good "at" beauty, rather than as relating to actual beauty. Michelle leaked beauty pageant secrets such as duct-taped breasts and adhesive sprayed to butts for swimsuit competitions. In some protests, Ann wore designer evening gowns made out of steaks with ribbons, as cops went nuts trying to keep their dogs off her. Streets were closed off, police had a full presence. And to top it all off, Ladies Against Women, a feminist street theater troupe out of San Francisco came down to "counterprotest" our protest, in wigs, horned rim glasses and furs, with hilarious handouts and signs saying things like "I'd rather be ironing." It was complete chaos. Finally the Miss California pageant moved to San Diego. And the Santa Cruz entourage followed in busloads.

What to Do About Weight Slavery

I once did a "body esteem for women" workshop at a resort, and the enrollees were all young, blonde women. I was stunned and then realized, of course, thin women live in as much, if not more weight slavery than fat women! It makes total sense.

People need to discuss how much of this body imagery stuff is just a product sold to us by industry. We are being brainwashed to hate our bodies so that we can buy unnecessary products to remedy them, and waste endless hours on artificial beauty. There is an argument to be made that beauty products, dieting and other body image consumerisms are diverting our attention from important things, like the economy, as much as any war does!

Guerrilla theater and activism help to counteract the negative imagery from the beauty industry, while entertaining and educating at the same time. International No Diet Day, May 6, is always a good day for activism. One year we put bookmarks that said "It's Okay to be Fat!" in diet books at the public library. Another year we sponsored a public sledge-hammering of bathroom scales. SeaFATtle has yearly No Diet Day events. Other forms of radical body activism are as simple as using cloth pads, like your granny did, for menstrual flows. Or not wearing commercial makeup on your face. Or not dieting because Jenny Craig is a tool of The Man! Take your body esteem out of the hands of corporate industries and realize that you are more beautiful than you ever imagined—today!

| *"The antibeauty critique engages in cultural cruelty."*

The Images of Beauty Do Not Hurt Women

Linda M. Scott

Linda M. Scott is an associate professor in the Institute of Communications Research at the University of Illinois and the author of Fresh Lipstick: Redressing Fashion and Feminism. *In the following viewpoint excerpted from* Fresh Lipstick, *Scott counters the feminist argument that the beauty and fashion industries, as well as the media images they create, oppress women. She states that beauty companies and fashion magazines are, in fact, dominated by women, not a patriarchy. Moreover, Scott declares that self-decoration—makeup, clothing, cosmetic surgery—is a fundamental form of human expression with different meanings to the individual. Therefore, feminists' promotion of a "natural" female appearance is their impulse to control women, the author concludes.*

As you read, consider the following questions:

1. In what ways did women in Afghanistan resist oppression, in the author's opinion?

Linda M. Scott, *Fresh Lipstick: Redressing Fashion and Feminism.* New York: Palgrave MacMillan, 2005. Copyright © Linda M. Scott, 2005. All rights reserved. Reproduced by permission.

2. How may the corsets worn by the Dinka tribe in Africa appear to Westerners?

3. What is the author's proposition to true feminists?

America sat transfixed. The images of the world news networks broke, rearranged themselves, and repeated, like pieces of glass in a kaleidoscope. Over and again two towers crumbled in smoke, dark-skinned people danced in a faraway street, and tense men in ties tried to explain. For the first few days, citizens of a wealthy, educated but insular nation learned about conditions in parts of the planet many had never even thought about. At the center of the lesson was the tragic state of Afghanistan. There, religious fundamentalists, having imposed their retrograde will on their own people, had now turned toward the West to avenge fear of a changing world.

Life under the Taliban, as glimpsed through the lens of CNN, was brutal. Most salient among the intolerable conditions was the treatment of women. Covered and cloistered, adult females were kept from interacting with the world in any way—and were horrifically punished if they broke through the wall of custom and law that held them. Denied education or employment, they were trapped in the despair of an elaborate system that, like many traditional patriarchies, was designed specifically to keep their sexuality contained so their bodies could be controlled and traded by men.

Within the framework of these shocking images, however, were two vignettes of resistance, two poignant gestures of courage and hope. On one hand were videos showing educated women secretly teaching girls. And on the other were films of women grooming other women in the styles of the West. Whether learning to read or learning to apply lipstick, these women, through these acts, were resisting their oppression and, in the process, risking their safety. None of these actions, however, was as dangerous as transgressing this order at its center—by giving your own self sexually to a man of your choosing. For that kind of resistance, the punishment was public execution.

Globally oriented feminists have tried for decades to shake America into awareness about the unspeakable circumstances of women around the world. Suddenly those conditions had literally hit home. Yet the high-relief illustration these clips provided of how limited American feminist thought was when it came to dress seemed to go unnoticed.

An Instrument of Revolution

A tube of lipstick as an instrument of revolution? A love affair as an act of resistance? A traditional economy more oppressive to women than any industrialized nation? There is nothing in the feminist ideology on grooming, kinship, or economics to account for these contradictions. And indeed, the more you look at it, the more contradictions there are: a culture where women are held in place by being "desexualized," not "sexualized"; a place where women are oppressed by *not* allowing men to ogle them. But in Afghanistan there is no fashion industry, no advertising.

There was also no advertising in the former Soviet Union. Yet the women coming forward from the ruins of that socialist state over the past decade have not reported their lives as a feminist utopia. In fact, the writings of newly emerged eastern European and Russian feminists often have clashed with the received view, causing those Americans who care to engage in the dialog to rethink some of their most basic assumptions about the nature of women's oppression.

The globalization of the Western economy, like the imperialism of the past, threatens tribal cultures in Africa and South America and in pockets all over the globe. In these small civilizations, we still see suggestions of the full extent of variation in human dress and grooming. And, as is often the case with cultures very different from our own, the practices still observable often turn our own assumptions upside down. The men of the Dinka tribe in Africa, for instance, wear elaborately beaded corsets (and little else) every day from puberty to old age. A few wealthy women are also allowed to wear them. To a Western eye, the tight, bright corsets look extremely uncomfortable and definitely "sexualizing." Yet they are clearly a mark of power and outline a stratification system only partly accounted for by gender. With the help of museum exhibitions, such as the one on body decoration held at the American Museum of Natural History in New York during 1999, Americans learn to look at the shaping and painting of the human body in other cultures as an art form. Yet even with glossy exhibition catalogs at our disposal, few of us can accord our own body decoration practices the same status.

Across the board, in fact, we seem to be unable to view our own dress practices for what they are: "a local example of the forms human life has locally taken." We paint our faces, pour ourselves into tight clothes, even undergo plastic surgery, as part of a long-standing and universal tradition in human behavior. As one anthropologist wrote: "There is no known culture in which people do not paint, pierce, tattoo, re-shape or simply adorn their bodies." Yet feminist ideology expects us to be different—and in this way, *better*—than the rest of humanity. By taking this position, the self-declared leaders of this movement push us into a way of dealing with life that is fundamentally inhumane. By ignoring the way that self-decoration expresses the human force of creative expression—the song of the self to come into being—and by denying the strength these practices can bring at moments of depression, dislocation, and even death, the antibeauty critique engages in cultural cruelty.

And this happens by way of an intellectual hoax. One of my strategies in researching and writing this book [*Fresh Lipstick: Redressing Fashion and Feminism*] was to take the sacred cows of the critique one by one and check them out against the historical record. A lot of the evidence I turned up directly contradicted what feminists were saying. As it turns out, blondes did *not* dominate the discourse on beauty, the fashion industry was *never* a patriarchy, the editors of the fashion magazines have *not* been mostly men, the most effective feminists in history have *not* all looked like clones of [civil rights activist] Susan B. Anthony. The ideas that feminists writing on this topic have advanced about the way pictures work, or the way people "naturally" dress, or the way advertising-free economies operate do *not* square with cross-cultural or historical evidence. In fact, the more I poked around at the feminist critique of fashion, the more aware I became that it has been constructed mostly of unsubstantiated assertions, many of which are flatly untrue but which get repeated, each feminist citing the other, until they take on lives of their own. What I also found, consistently, were phenomena considerably more complex, problematic, and intelligent than the critique allowed.

The "Natural" Position

Perhaps the most dishonest aspect of this critique is the way it asserts the "natural" position, the philosophical "God's eye view." A woman in a pair of blue jeans and a T-shirt arriving in Taliban-controlled Afghanistan (or any number of other places around the world) is not "natural" and certainly not politically neutral, regardless of how little makeup she may wear on her face. The same woman is no more natural at home in the United States just because we are accustomed to looking at her. And she occupies no less interested a position here than abroad. All human dress speaks of social order and therefore is *never* politically neutral.

The feminists' preemption of a "natural" position on dress is, as I expect my readers to recognize now, possible *only* because of their superior status vis-à-vis other women (those whose dress they try to control). The impulse to reform the

A Girl-Powered Industry

Names like Helena Rubinstein, Elizabeth Arden, Madam C.J. Walker, Estee Lauder, and Mary Kay Ash are still recognized to this day, nearly a century after starting their own companies. And though entrepreneurs like Hazel Bishop and Annie Tumbo Malone may be less well-known, they were responsible for the development of smudge-free lipstick and African-American-centric cosmetics, respectively—no small feats (and evidence of some great business minds).

But women's leadership in makeup dates back . . . further than the word "feminism" itself. Though Egyptians were known to use kohl (an early form of eyeliner/mascara) and Native Americans were recognized for their plant-infused formulas meant to fix facial flaws, the majority of cosmetic recipes are traced back to Queen Elizabeth and other women of the Victorian era.

Kate Ward, "Makeup Is a Feminist Act,"
Sirens, September 2008.

dress of others is an extension of the historical trajectory of appearance in America. In this sartorial history, higher moral value has been given to certain modes of dress—simple, colorless, asexual—largely because of their associations with certain groups: the Puritans of the colonial period, Yankee Protestants of the early Industrial Revolution, scholastic suffragists from the turn of the century, neo-Puritans of the Jazz Age, and neo-Marxists of the Second Wave. Other groups have had more colorful ways of dressing and have been just as important to the feminist movement, but histories of American feminism have overlooked them. Still in the shadows are the penny capitalists of the early fashion and beauty industry, actresses of both stage and screen, lesbians, women of the old West, witches, the "flower children" of the 1960s, and a substantial variety of "ethnic" women. Without a doubt, these women had a different viewpoint on the politics of dress than did the Puritan feminists. Are we prepared to say their views were, categorically, less valid?

The continuing refusal by feminists writing on this topic to consider other viewpoints suggests that they don't believe another legitimate opinion or experience exists. Thus they claim for themselves the "view from nowhere": a philosophical position that is absolutely true and objective, the single viewpoint from which all is clear, all is known, and nothing is assailable. Ironically, feminists once used this phrase to describe the viewpoint asserted by white, prosperous males (a.k.a. "the patriarchy"). One of the most difficult and important tasks of early Second Wave intellectual feminism was to argue against the notion that the male view was the only right, objective way to look at the world. Feminists had to show—and *did* show—that gender makes a difference in a person's experience and therefore constructs another viewpoint that, although equally legitimate, affects estimations of what is rational, good, fair, moral, or even true.

By the 1990s, white intellectual feminists were being criticized for having asserted their own view from nowhere. In response, [feminist philosopher] Susan Bordo wrote that people who propose to focus attention on the particularities of dress, rather than admitting to the obvious reality of the matter in general terms (that is to say, the truth as viewed from nowhere), are merely indulging in a fantasy she dubs "the dream of everywhere." The problem with the view from everywhere, she argues, is that it fragments the feminist critique, degenerating into facile "celebrations" of diversity and leaving the movement weakened.

A View from Elsewhere

This book *is* intended as an attack on the true feminist's "God's eye view" of dress. But it is *not* some sloppy dream of seeing "from everywhere." Instead, my proposal is more modest: I am simply suggesting that true feminists consider the possibility of a view from *elsewhere*. The politics of dress that I have described in this book is one with which we can recognize multiple strategies, differing origins, and various aspirations, and thus has a sharper edge for analyzing the power relations expressed through dress than simply breaking the world down into a false, self-interested idea of "natural" versus everything else. By explaining this, I hope I have convinced some true feminists to show a little more humility and lot more compassion toward the dress of other women. By demonstrating how much the meaning of dress and grooming habits varies according to each woman's place in race, class, and history, I hoped to sensitize all my readers to the need to reserve judgment on such matters until they have considered them thoughtfully and with the benefit of a reasonable amount of evidence to support their theories.

In the end, I hope I have encouraged others who are dedicated to the equality of women, but who do not wish to give up the pleasures of self-decoration, to renew their commitment to the project of feminism. Voices from around the world report a variety of conditions and systems under which only one thing holds constant: the universal second-class status of females. If there was ever a moment when the women of one culture had a responsibility toward their sisters in other nations, this is it. We should not waste time quibbling over what to wear to the conflict. Instead, I would hope that, armed with a new perspective, a rejuvenated resolve, and, yes, even a little fresh lipstick, American feminism could venture out into the world to meet the challenge.

| "An experienced hiring hand will ignore good looks, right? Not exactly."

Beautiful People Have Advantages in the Workplace

Gordon L. Patzer

Gordon L. Patzer is the founding director of the Appearance Research Institute in Chicago, Illinois, and the author of Looks: Why They Matter More Than You Ever Imagined. *In the following viewpoint excerpted from* Looks, *Patzer insists that physical attractiveness brings several advantages to the workplace. Patzer maintains that a job applicant's good looks give him or her an edge over similarly and better-qualified candidates. In addition, he claims that attractive employees are paid more and hold higher positions than their plainer counterparts. And physical attractiveness benefits the bottom line, according to Patzer: companies with good-looking executives yield higher revenues than those with average-looking executives.*

As you read, consider the following questions:

1. What studies does the author cite to support his claim that attractive, tall people receive higher pay?

2. How does Patzer respond to the assertion that better-looking executives apply to the most successful companies?

3. What is the one disadvantage of being an attractive employee, as stated by Patzer?

So you're good-looking. Neonatal nurses nurtured you nonstop upon your arrival in this world. Your parents handed you everything a kid could want, and way more. Teachers from preschool and kindergarten all the way through college and grad school bent backward and forward to cut you every break possible. But now here you are, out of school and about to interview for your first job. So put all that stuff behind you and get real, young sir or miss, because this is the workplace. The gig. The grind. The rat race. Here in Nine-to-Five City, stockholders insist on profits and bosses expect you to work hard to inflate their bonuses. The bottom line *is* the bottom line. Do you really think that anybody, from the executive suite to the factory floor, gives a flying flip about how beautiful you are?

Well, yes, they do.

And quite a bit.

The fact is, if you are competing for a position against candidates who seem to possess exactly the same qualifications, but *you* are very attractive while the others are average or less in the PA [physical attractiveness] department, scientific studies say that you will get the job and they will not. Always? Well, if you're bursting with PA but could use a manicure or even a minor makeover while the competition is well groomed but so-so looking, relax—you've still got the edge. Your good looks help most when you and your competitors are all otherwise run-of-the-mill candidates: If another applicant is exceptionally well qualified but you're not, you may get a follow-up interview but probably not the job.

A Clear Linkage

The data and studies that form the scientific basis for this hire-the-handsome phenomenon have been available to personnel managers and corporate management for decades. Most human resource [HR] types are well aware that signing the guy with the toothpaste-ad smile or the gorgeous gal with the gams up to *here* isn't solid management practice. An experienced hiring hand will ignore good looks, right?

Not exactly. Yes, the science is readily available and many seasoned hiring executives have actually read it. And no, it doesn't seem to make much difference. Even though they *believe* that they are able to overlook an applicant's PA, and even as they sincerely insist that they ignore such superficialities when making hiring decisions, many experienced managers will end up selecting an applicant with high PA whose job qualifications merely match or parallel those of a less attractive candidate. That's because they think the person with high PA is actually *better* qualified or, if not, will nevertheless turn into a better employee.

And short men, along with all PA-challenged women, no matter how qualified, start any job interview with strikes against them, even when the hiring decision is made by a highly experienced manager or HR executive.

In 2000, British economist Barry Harper examined voluminous data relating to over 11,000 people born in Britain in 1958 and concluded that both men and women "assessed as unattractive or short experience a significant earnings penalty. Tall men receive a pay premium while obese women experience a pay penalty." Harper concluded that while there was evidence that short men and ugly women were on infrequent occasion less productive, "the bulk of the pay differential for appearance arises from employer discrimination."

Oh yes, that's England! But here in the land of the free and the home of the brave? Would an American company really discriminate against a job applicant because he was short? Against a woman who was, shall we say, not so attractive?

Darn tootin' they do, and a pair of Yank professors have the goods to prove it. Daniel M. Cable, a business professor at the University of North Carolina, Chapel Hill, and Timothy A. Judge, professor of management at the University of Florida, studied data from 8,590 individuals in four different studies in both Great Britain and the United States. These studies followed thousands of participants from childhood to adulthood and examined many details of both their work and their personal lives.

Cable and Judge found no important difference between employees in the United Kingdom and the United States; in both countries their data document a clear linkage between physical height and career success. A person's altitude, they learned, is a significant predictor of attitudes expressed toward them. Height flavors the way people dole out social esteem, invest in leadership, and rate performance, especially in men. . . .

If you are happily among the good-looking and have a job, over the long haul—and most likely, over the short term, too—you will probably be paid more than average-looking counterparts and you will probably rise to a higher level in the organization than those with less PA. Studies show that physically attractive people tend to have better-paying jobs in higher-level positions than do their less attractive counterparts.

How much more? Evidence from studies conducted in the United States, Canada, and China in 1994 and 1999 suggests that highly attractive employees enjoy increased earnings of between 7.5 percent and 15 percent over their average-looking peers.

Why will a bottom-line business shell out more moola to those oozing PA if how they *look* doesn't make any difference in how well they do their job? Is it merely discrimination

Higher Pay for Attractive Workers

Attractive people earn about 5 percent more in hourly pay than their average-looking colleagues, who in turn earn 9 percent more per hour than the plainest-looking workers.

This means if an average-looking person earned $40,000, their prettiest co-workers would make $42,000, while their least attractive colleagues brought home just $36,400.

Laura Morsch, "Looks Matter in the Workplace,"
CareerBuilder.com (Posted February 28, 2007).

against the PA impaired, or does hiring good-looking people increase productivity or somehow help to bring in more bucks?

Beauty Capital

To find out, economists Gerard A. Pfann of Holland's University of the Maastricht; Jeff E. Biddle, Michigan State University; Daniel S. Hamermesh, University of Texas, Austin; and Ciska M. Bosman of Nice, France, conducted a study focused on the looks of executives in Holland's busy and highly competitive advertising industry. Pfann and his colleagues collected data from hundreds of Dutch advertising firms to analyze the effect of employees' attractiveness, or beauty, on their firms' performance.

They began by assuming that all else being equal, in an industry where employees frequently interact with clients, firms with more attractive workers will face less customer discrimination and thus gain a competitive advantage. But to make a difference on the bottom line of a balance sheet, the beauty of employees must have some measurable positive effect, both on the agency's production of revenue and on its profits after expenses. So, if an agency with beautiful workers pays them *more* than not-so-beautiful workers of equal ability, the company must somehow bring in not merely enough extra income to offset the expense of higher salaries and fringe benefits, but still more income to cover the expense of finding and hiring good-looking people and keeping other, less physically attractive workers motivated—and even more income to increase profit.

The income generated by employee labor is known as "quasi-rents," and according to economic theory, if quasi-rents increase with employee ability, profits may be increased by employing more able or productive workers.

In advertising firms, good working relationships among co-workers and with clients create a type of "human capital," and good ways to create these relationships lower the cost of acquiring this capital. So, more beautiful managers may find it easier to develop relationships with other employees and clients, generating higher earnings for themselves and higher quasi-rents for their company. All else being equal, firms with more beauty capital will produce more and obtain higher revenues. This was the theory that the data would either prove or debunk.

To begin their study, Pfann and his colleagues collected photos of the top management of 289 Dutch ad agencies, and then billing and earnings data from those agencies over a twelve-year span starting in 1984. Collectively, the agencies' sales volume represented about 70 percent of all ad industry revenue in the Netherlands—a very sizable sample.

Executive beauty was assessed using 1,282 black-and-white photos—head-and-shoulders shots from industry yearbooks—an average of 2.71 pictures per firm. These photos were rated independently by a panel of two men and one woman aged 40 or older, and by a second panel of two men and one woman aged 39 or younger. (The makeup of these panels reflected the age-sex distribution of the ad agencies' clientele.) The people in the photos were rated on a five-point scale, where 5 was "strikingly handsome or beautiful" and 1 was "homely."

The panel rated the average ad-agency manager at 2.80, or just below average in PA. And, as expected, executive beauty had a positive effect on revenue. After taking into account such factors as the size and location of the agency and its experience in the industry, whether small or large, all but a few agencies with better-looking executives reported significantly higher revenue.

Beauty Brings Success

But hold on! Does beauty really bring success? What if it's the other way around—success attracts beauty? What if better-looking executives are attracted to join successful agencies *because* these firms bring in more revenue? By tracking employment records, Pfann and his colleagues found no evidence to support this notion: Previously successful firms did *not* attract better-looking executives.

In fact, the Dutch study showed that beauty is highly productive. Among all firms sampled, those with better-looking executives brought in an average of 120,000 guilders more per year in billing revenue. And aside from a handful of tiny agencies operating in Holland's most competitive business region, known as the Randstad, firms boasting better-looking management averaged an extra 188,000 guilders per year in revenue. (The study identified several very small firms, all operating in Holland's most competitive advertising environment, that lacked the financial resources or management ability to capitalize on having a few executives with higher-than-average PA.)

And how much better looking were the men and women who run top-earning firms than those of the average Dutch agency manager? Pfann and friends calculated that the most successful firms employed managers whose beauty was greater than that of ninety out of every hundred Dutch ad executives.

And now to the bottom line. What was the return on this investment of beauty capital? By massaging their Dutch data and estimating individual executive salaries based on industry data, Pfann calculated that good-looking execs created significantly more income from quasi-rents than they cost their companies in higher wages. Even though their own salaries substantially exceeded industry averages, their agencies earned even more. "Beauty capital yields returns to both workers and firms," concluded Pfann and his colleagues. . . .

A Higher Penalty

While PA in business can spell "personal asset" to those who have it, those high in PA must also shoulder the burden of their bosses' higher expectations or jealousy—and when the boss is frustrated or disappointed, they pay a higher penalty for personal indiscretions than their more ordinary-looking colleagues.

This was the conclusion of a 2002 study by a psychology professor and a pair of undergraduate students at North Central College, in the Chicago suburb of Naperville. They assembled a group of ninety-eight students, including thirty-six MBA [master of business administration] candidates, and asked them to act as "managers" in evaluating the actions of "employees" who violated a company policy against using company computers to access the Internet to shop.

Based on the data, Professor Karl Kelley and students Lori Nita and Brittain Bandura were able to observe how a manager's decision to punish an employee policy violator was affected by the employee's gender and PA. Their data revealed that attractive females were punished most harshly and attractive males suffered the least severe consequences. When it came to employees with low PA, however, the violator's gender made no difference.

What's going on here? Why would managers come down harder on an attractive woman than an ordinary-looking one who had committed the same offense? Probably because business has a sort of love-hate relationship with beauty. Driven by ideals of fairness, or maybe envy, ill will can smolder against coworkers thought to have attained employment unjustly. Better-looking females are known particularly to be the target of such speculations. Managers are not insensitive to these dynamics and, to avoid accusations about preferential treatment, they can feel compelled to mete out stronger disciplinary action when a presumably preferred employee violates company rules. Their doing so is backhanded recognition that their PA opens many doors that remain closed to more average-looking people. Some managers therefore tend to hold their better-looking employees, whom they suspect have always gotten the breaks, more accountable for behaviors that have negative effects on the organization. . . .

So you're good-looking, and just as your exceptional looks have opened many doors for you, you get this job—even though you were no better prepared for it than other candidates. If you keep your new job, you can expect a bigger salary and faster promotions than the average worker here. If you hope one day to rise to the top of your new company, you've got a good shot—but if you screw up, you can also expect to be treated more harshly than your fellow employees.

And as you get older, you will have to work harder and harder to hang on to your looks. So good luck.

> "People are more likely to trust a pretty face, but when that trust is betrayed, the backlash can be ugly."

Beautiful People May Not Have Advantages in the Workplace

Jennifer Chamberlain

In the following viewpoint, Jennifer Chamberlain states that while having good looks may bring more income and prestige in the workplace, they also come with a penalty. People have very high expectations and are more trusting of attractive individuals, but according to Chamberlain, a recent study shows that the reactions are harsher when expectations are not met. To resolve how snap judgments based on physical appearance affect promotions and scapegoating on the job, companies can help employees develop their interpersonal skills, the author writes. Chamberlain is business editor and producer at Dallasnews.com, the Web site of the Dallas Morning News.

Jennifer Chamberlain, "Study Finds 'Beauty Penalty' Can Be Harsh," *Dallas Morning News* (dallasnews.com), October 2, 2006. Reprinted with permission of the *Dallas Morning News*.

As you read, consider the following questions:

1. As stated by Chamberlain, what are the advantages of being physically attractive at work?

2. According to the author, what happened in the study when attractive subjects returned fewer "lab dollars" than expected?

3. What is Catherine Eckel's "takeaway message" about beauty?

People are more likely to trust a pretty face, but when that trust is betrayed, the backlash can be ugly, according to a study published recently by Rice University.

Numerous studies have shown that attractive people generally make more money, get higher reviews from their supervisors, and are viewed as being more intelligent and trustworthy. What surprised researchers in this study was that subjects deemed attractive also were penalized more harshly for failing to live up to expectations.

"There's a lot of work in experimental economics and in other aspects of economics like labor economics where they find that attractive people have a beauty premium," said Catherine Eckel, a professor of economics at the University of Texas at Dallas, who co-authored the study with Rice professor Rick Wilson.

"It's kind of a pervasive thing, but the twist that we have in our paper that you don't see in the others is this 'beauty penalty,'" she said. "What we see in our data is that people have very high expectations of attractive people, and when they're disappointed, they react."

In the study called "Judging a Book by Its Cover: Beauty and Expectations in the Trust Game," 206 university students were asked to participate in a series of "trust games."

Each student was given 10 "lab dollars." Then they were told they could send any amount of the money to other stu-

Explaining the Premium of Beauty

[Researchers D.] Hamermesh and [J.] Biddle found that there is some sorting of beautiful people into occupations in which employers report that looks may increase productivity, such as in sales, but that this is not strong enough to explain much of the premium to beauty. This leaves social effects rather than productivity effects as the natural place to look for explanations. Our research suggests one effect of beauty is rooted in stereotypes. Beautiful people tend to be in more successful teams because other team members are more cooperative in the presence of beautiful people. This is true when effort is not observable, and suggests that a beauty premium may be more likely to exist when productivity is not perfectly observed, implying that beautiful people may also sort into occupations where individual productivity is difficult to measure.

James Andreoni and Ragan Petrie,
"Beauty, Gender, and Stereotypes:
Evidence from Laboratory Experiments,"
Journal of Economic Psychology, *29, 2008.*

dents, making their choices based on photographs. The study moderators then tripled the amount sent to the recipients, who were allowed to decide how much to refund to the sender, also based only on photographs.

A separate group of students evaluated the pictures for a number of traits, including attractiveness.

The researchers found that, on average, the students deemed attractive received more money and also tended to reciprocate more generously.

However, initial recipients also expected more cash from the attractive students, and when they received less, punished them more harshly by skimping on the returned money.

"Human beings make decisions based on stereotypes, it's like a shorthand way of making judgments, and when we do that, we make mistakes," Ms. Eckel said.

And those mistakes can have broad social and economic consequences.

"For example, suppose that when you have an opportunity to have an interaction with somebody, you're more likely to pick someone who is of one type rather than another. Then as you begin to aggregate that to the whole economy, what you might see is that people of that other type don't get as many opportunities to interact as people of the first type," Ms. Eckel explained.

This, in turn, can reduce economic opportunities and become a mechanism for discrimination, she said.

John Challenger, chief executive of Chicago outplacement firm Challenger, Gray & Christmas, said there's no doubt perceptions of attractiveness are among many factors in workplace relationships. "That then impacts promotions and terminations and scapegoating and other kinds of behaviors that take place every day," he said.

The good news is that workers who recognize those factors and raise what Mr. Challenger refers to as EQ, or emotional intelligence, can give them an advantage in resolving issues that might arise based on snap judgments.

"In big, complex organizations, interpersonal skill and knowledge is a great benefit to those who possess it. So if you know that people are reacting to you in an inauthentic way because of your appearance, you can seek solutions to those issues. .... Sometimes that may mean avoiding those people, sometimes it may mean coming to terms with them. It takes more effort to break down those barriers or try different solutions," he said.

Mr. Challenger said he's seen a trend of companies working to address interpersonal relationships and build common ground among employees, through executive coaching and other programs.

"So I think companies are recognizing that EQ is not just innate but also can be a learned behavior," he said.

Ms. Eckel said her research has also shown that the only way to change stereotypes is to be aware of them. And, as it turns out, our mothers may have been right when they told us that "pretty is as pretty does."

"The takeaway message here is that people have the wrong idea about attractiveness," she said. "Attractive people, well, they're not less trustworthy than other people, but they're not more trustworthy either. So if we're aware of our biases, we can do a little better job of making decisions."

Periodical Bibliography

The following articles have been selected to supplement the diverse views presented in this chapter.

Geraldine Bedell — "What Makes Women Happy?" *Guardian*, June 11, 2006.

Susannah Cullinane — "When Being Tall Is a 'Disability,'" *BBC News*, September 11, 2005.

Umberto Eco — "What's Ugly?" *Los Angeles Times*, November 18, 2007.

Robin Givhan — "Channeling the Ideal of Modern Beauty," *Washington Post*, March 8, 2009.

Ling Liu Injae Hwang, Chan Yong Kim, Scarlet Ma, and Michiko Toyama — "Mirror, Mirror . . ." *Time International* (Asia Edition), October 31, 2005.

Sarah Kershaw — "Move Over My Pretty, Ugly Is Here," *New York Times*, October 30, 2008.

Marianna Macdonald — "The Wages of Beauty Are Loneliness," *Spectator*, February 2, 2008.

Taryn Plumb — "In Opposing 'Heightism,' She Has Found Her Cause," *Boston Globe*, January 17, 2008.

Scott Reeves — "Good Looks, Good Pay?" *Forbes*, May 5, 2005.

Liz Wolgesmith — "How Plastic Surgery Can Boost Your Career," *U.S. News & World Report*, May 12, 2008.

OPPOSING VIEWPOINTS® SERIES

CHAPTER 3

Should People Strive for Beauty?

Chapter Preface

In 2008, more than 160,000 people eighteen years old and younger had surgical and nonsurgical cosmetic procedures. This accounts for 2 percent of the 10.2 million cases performed in the United States that year, according to the American Society for Aesthetic Plastic Surgery (ASAPS). Rhinoplasty, or nose jobs, were the most popular surgical enhancement among this age group, ASAPS reports, while laser hair removal was the leading nonsurgical procedure. Also, it is becoming more common for teens to have liposuction, breast augmentation, and Botox injections.

Because of their ongoing physical and emotional development and the associated health risks, teens and cosmetic procedures is a hot-button issue. Physician and *Los Angeles Times* columnist Valerie Ulene claims, "They face tremendous pressure to be attractive, and they're constantly bombarded with images of beautiful men and women who are held up as the norm. . . . [A]ltering the way you look before you're even done developing physically seems almost ridiculous."[1] Others are doubtful of the self-image boost they supposedly provide. "Although patients who have undergone a cosmetic procedure often do feel better about that particular body part," says Diana Zuckerman, president of the National Research Center for Women & Families, "there's really no data to suggest that it improves their overall body image or self-esteem."[2]

Yet, other health care professionals contend that cosmetic procedures for adolescents should be determined on a case-by-case basis and surgeries such as breast reduction and otoplasty (for protruding or abnormally large ears) can bring significant physical and emotional benefits. Before the teen goes under the knife, the American Society of Plastic Surgeons (ASPS) recommends that he or she initially requests the procedure, has grounded expectations, and can handle the healing process. The authors in the following chapter deliberate upon the often controversial pursuit of beauty.

Notes

1. *Los Angeles Times*, January 12, 2009.
2. *Los Angeles Times*, January 12, 2009.

> "It's nonsense on one level, of course, but the power of lipstick, and how it makes a woman feel, must never be trivialised."

Cosmetics Can Enhance Physical Appearances and Self-Esteem

Annalisa Barbieri

In the following viewpoint, Annalisa Barbieri argues that cosmetics are not just ways to improve one's looks, but are essential to a woman's self-esteem. A simple, everyday task such as putting on lipstick may be trivial, claims the author, but the impact on a woman's psyche should not be underestimated. Barbieri asserts that cosmetics are especially empowering for women who have recently been through a traumatic experience, such as victims of beatings by their partners or, in an extreme case, survivors of a concentration camp. Annalisa Barbieri previously worked in fashion PR and wrote about fashion for several British newspapers before writing for the New Statesman.

Annalisa Barbieri, "Purely Cosmetic?" *New Statesman*, April 2, 2007, p. 52. Reproduced by permission.

As you read, consider the following questions:

1. What are the two cosmetics that most women say they cannot live without?

2. What did John Gustafson do with the excess, unused makeup that he got in the course of his job as a skin-care guru?

3. How did lipstick help the liberated survivors of Bergen-Belsen in 1945?

A woman's handbag is, quite rightly, a mystery. But within the folds of fluff and amid the wraps of paper that register phone numbers of unimaginable importance, there is something of such value that it could be described as the beating heart of the handbag: the make-up bag.

It takes time to build a cosmetics purse. Sure, you can go to those shiny counters, staffed by women whose eyebrows are tamed beyond any possibility of revolt, and spend a couple of hundred pounds, and you would, indeed, end up with a fully staffed make-up bag. It wouldn't be yours, though—and it won't be, until the lipstick has been worked down into a shape that exactly fits your lips, and until the eyebrow colours in their neat-no-more palette have been broken down to make them more malleable, and therefore easier to apply.

In terms of status in among the cosmetics, the lipstick is queen. Lipsticks have had entire books dedicated to them. Next is mascara. These are the two items most women say they cannot live without. It's nonsense on one level, of course, but the power of lipstick, and how it makes a woman feel, must never be trivialised. From the silly everyday occurrence— the woman having to "put her lippy on" before a relatively difficult exchange—to the enormous impact make-up and lipstick can have on a woman's psyche, there's more going on than just colouring in one's face.

A Makeup Artist's Perspective

I think people are now more aware of taking up makeup as a profession, as compared to [2003 or 2004]. I've been in the industry myself for three years now . . . .

As for what inspired me to get into it, I love to make people look their best—it appeals to me to help someone make the most of their looks. Confidence comes into most people as a result and my work is appreciated.

Rediff News *with Dilshad Ukaji,*
"My Work Instills Self-Confidence in People," May 22, 2008.

Cosmetics Help Women After Traumatic Experiences

The skincare guru John Gustafson shocked me one day by telling me how he gave all the excess (unused) make-up he got in the course of his job to a women's refuge. It seemed a frivolous, almost insulting, thing to offer women who had been beaten by their partners; but apparently it was a huge help psychologically for the women, many of whom had had to leave their homes with very little.

Some years ago I read this powerful extract from the diary of Lieutenant Colonel Mervin Willett Gonin, one of the first British soldiers to liberate Bergen-Belsen in 1945. (I have verified the source from the Imperial War Museum.)

"I can give no adequate description of the Horror Camp in which my men and myself were to spend the next month of our lives . . . It was shortly after the British Red Cross arrived, though it may have no connection, that a very large quantity of lipstick arrived. This was not at all what we men wanted. We were screaming for hundreds and thousands of other things and I don't know who asked for lipstick. I wish so much that I could discover who did it. It was the action of genius, sheer unadulterated brilliance. I believe nothing did more for these internees than the lipstick ... At last someone had done something to make them individuals again: they were someone, no longer merely the number tattooed on the arm. At last they could take an interest in their appearance. That lipstick started to give them back their humanity."

> "You're almost certainly hotter than you think. It's partly a matter of limited attention—everyone else is too fixated on his or her own appearance to be critical of yours."

Individuals Should Focus on Self-Acceptance

Carlin Flora

In the following viewpoint, Carlin Flora argues that people are not objective when judging their own looks and are more beautiful than they think they are. People may zero-in on imperfections that others don't see, because everyone else is too worried about their own appearance to notice, contends Flora. Understanding your own self-perceptions is the key to stopping the obsession about your looks, asserts Flora, and can actually make you look better by improving your confidence. Carlin Flora is a senior editor for Psychology Today *magazine.*

As you read, consider the following questions:

    1. What is the "contrast effect"?

Carlin Flora, "The Beguiling Truth About Beauty," *Psychology Today*, May–June 2006, pp. 62–72. Reproduced by permission.

2. How do people who score high on measures of the "public self-consciousness" personality trait judge themselves?

3. How are our "internal mirrors" shaped by our parents?

Don't hate yourself for wanting to be beautiful. Good-looking people get special treatment from strangers, employers and even their own mothers. The comely reap real social and economic gains in life, from broader romantic proposals to lighter punishment in criminal courts. The rest of us curse the advantages of beauty because we can never claim membership in the knockout club.

Or can we? We're not even close to objective when it comes to judging our own looks. Other people see the whole package. But when we look in the mirror, we're liable to zero in on the imperfections. That bump on your friend's nose? It's her trademark! It gives her character! But to you, that thing on your nose is downright disfiguring. Our opinion of our own looks is also capricious: We can feel like the belle of the ball at one party, but downright shabby at the next, all on the same night.

So if we can't trust our own self-appraisal, or the reassurances of friends and family, we're left to the cool judgment of strangers to satisfy our curiosity about our appearance. The Web site "Hot or Not," which lets people anonymously submit their photos for others to rate on a 10-point scale, had nearly 2 million daily page views within a week of launching in 2000. Not exactly the best way to bolster your self-image.

Understanding Your Self-Perceptions

The good news: You're almost certainly hotter than you think. It's partly a matter of limited attention—everyone else is too fixated on his or her own appearance to be critical of yours. If you are particularly attentive to your body (as women tend to be), or if you feel uncomfortable in public, you are almost definitely hotter than you think. And we all have the innate ability to change how other people perceive us, without a physical transformation of any kind. When you're convinced you look good, others see you in a more favorable light. Call it an internal makeover: Understanding your own powerful self-perceptions can help you stop obsessing over your appearance—and look better.

Why is it that our self-judgments shift like weather on a spring day? Even a stroll down a street can change the way you think about your looks. Our brains have a built-in hot-or-not meter that never stops gathering data.

Psychologists call it the "contrast effect": You feel prettier around ugly people and uglier around pretty people. These social comparisons happen not only when you deliberately scrutinize passersby, but constantly and automatically. In one study, people given a subliminal glimpse of an attractive female face subsequently rated themselves as less attractive than those who saw a homely one, though no one remembered having seen the images at all. Our self-concepts are built on thousands of these comparisons.

"I'm five feet tall and I'm curvy. I feel good about how I look," says Deanna Melluso, a New York City-based makeup artist who dolls up models for magazine shoots and runway shows. "But when I'm around tall, thin women all day, I start to feel fat. As soon as I walk outside, I feel normal again—I see that I've been in a fake world."

Perhaps because their social status is often contingent upon their faces and bodies, women are particularly susceptible to this effect. "When women evaluate their physical attractiveness, they compare themselves with an idealized standard of beauty, such as a fashion model," says Richard Robins, professor of psychology at the University of California, Davis. "In contrast, when both men and women evaluate their intelligence, they do not compare themselves to Einstein, but rather to a more mundane standard."

In a study where people were asked to solve math problems, there was no difference in how well men and women scored—when everyone was fully dressed. But when subjects were required to perform the calculations in their bathing suits, the women suddenly fared worse than their male counterparts. They were too busy wondering how they looked to crunch numbers correctly.

Everyone judges his or her own appearance more critically when self-aware, as when giving a presentation to coworkers. But people who score high on measures of a personality trait called "public self-consciousness" feel that way all the time. We all know someone like this—a friend who never runs out of the house to grab coffee without fixing herself up first. Strangers generally consider such people to be more physically attractive than average, says William Thornton, professor of psychology at the University of Maine. But that extra personal care doesn't correct their internal funhouse mirrors: They tend to compare themselves exclusively with very good-looking people—and feel especially down after doing so.

As our faces and figures evolve during childhood and adolescence, we create a picture of ourselves that is hard to get out of our minds in adulthood, however outdated or wrong it may be. Not all people who grow up disliking their appearance were ugly children, says James Rosen, *emeritus* professor of psychology at the University of Vermont. Some were perfectly cute as kids, but had an exceptional trait, like being very tall or heavily freckled, which drew comments and stares.

Our "internal mirrors" are often shaped by our parents, contends psychoanalyst Vivian Diller. A child whose parents tell him he's ugly will have to overcome that perception, but that's uncommon. More subtle is the effect of "the gleam in their eye," says Diller—whether parents sincerely light up at the sight of us and appreciate our individual charms.

While parental love can bolster self-esteem for some, there's no direct line between childhood experiences and adult self-image. Ugly ducklings sometimes turn into swans—or find their looks suddenly validated by committee. Donelle Ruwe, now an English professor at Northern Arizona University, grew up terribly gawky, a teen with glasses, a back brace and, yes, even headgear. But she played piano very well. At the age of 19, she'd recently shed the brace, and a pageant scout looking to improve the talent quotient in a beauty competition suggested she sign up. She did, and was crowned Miss Meridian, Iowa, of 1985.

"For the first time, I felt that I was attractive," she says. That new confidence in her looks actually made her feel freer to develop her intellect—she was quicker to assert her opinions in class and debate with others. "I think that when you are self-conscious about your body, too much of your mind and emotions are focused on it," she says. "But once you let go of that self-consciousness, you can interact without it getting in the way."

Being Attractive Has Its Own Set of Problems

But those who are gorgeous from the get-go face their own set of potential problems. Very attractive kids may grow up to be insecure adults, especially if they were praised solely for their appearance. They may develop a particularly harsh way of assessing themselves—what Heather Patrick, a researcher at Baylor College of Medicine, calls "contingent self-esteem." They may feel good about their looks only if they meet a specific, and usually very high, expectation, such as weighing in at a certain number. Self-satisfaction is not on a spectrum for such people: If they don't meet their standard, they feel absolutely ugly.

Carol Alt, the former *Sports Illustrated* cover girl, fell victim to this phenomenon in 1995, when a fashion photographer declared her too jiggly for her bikini. After he spent a

FACIAL ÆSTHETICS

"WHAT'S HAPPENED TO MISS HIPPO? SHE SEEMS CHANGED."
"HAVEN'T YOU HEARD? SHE'S HAD HER FACE LIFTED."

Used with permission of the Ohio State University Treasury of Fine Arts, Cartoon Library and Museum.

day on location attempting to hide her extra ounces of flesh behind rocks, he fired her and sent her back to Los Angeles, where she slipped into a weeks-long, Nyquil-soaked depression. "I'd feel fat and guilty anytime I ate," she says now. "I didn't feel I had control over my body, and that fragility was frustrating and even terrifying."

With looks, as in other domains of life, we relish recognition more and recover better from failure when we believe that good results come from effort and not just from what God gave us. If you are born lovely, you have only your parents' genetic contributions to thank. But if you become more attractive because you've invested energy in taking good care of yourself, the credit is all yours.

Alt says she feels better-looking now, at 45, than she ever has. The author of *Eating in the Raw* says that overhauling her diet made the difference. "Now I'm more complimented when someone comments on something I've worked for, such as keeping myself healthy, than when someone says, 'You're beautiful.'"

Charm Can Trump Beauty

Ultimately, good looks aren't just a question of a lucky birth. In real life—outside the artificial bounds of lab tests and "hot or not" snapshots—our physical appearance is always evaluated alongside our body language, voice and temperament. Charm can trump beauty. In one study, psychologists videotaped people as they entered a room and introduced themselves to two people. They then asked strangers to rate the videotaped subjects on physical attractiveness, emotional expressiveness and social skills. All three qualities contributed to the subjects' overall likeability—but attractiveness was the least important factor.

The easiest way to influence how others view you is to demonstrate that you like them, say Ann Demarais and Valerie White, psychologists and authors of *First Impressions: What You Don't Know About How Others See You*. If you express interest in what others say, or smile and lightly touch their arm, they will likely feel flattered, comfortable around you and even more attracted to you. A person who finds you likeable will probably never notice your imperfections—besides, no one is as interested in your bald head or fleshy thighs as you are. Demarais and White tell of a client who suffered from the "spotlight illusion"—he imagined that people were homing in on his crooked teeth, which were his least favorite feature. Realizing that other people didn't really care about his teeth was freeing. "He experimented with smiling broadly when he met new people," they write. "When no one reacted in horror, and in fact responded positively, he began to feel at ease with his smile. When he seemed more comfortable in his own skin, he became more appealing to others."

Most of us have had the mysterious experience of watching a loved one become increasingly beautiful with time, as the relationship grows deeper. Imagine that generous gaze is upon you all the time, and you'll soon see a better reflection in others' eyes. You may not be able to turn off your inner hot-or-not meter, but you can spend less time fretting in the mirror and more time engaging with the world.

> *"A young woman ... explained that eye-shaping surgery 'wasn't a vanity thing. It really was this belief that if you looked a little more Western and a little less Asian, it's like having a great degree from a better school. ... It was something to put in your portfolio.'"*

Cosmetic Surgery Is Used to Alter Ethnic Characteristics

Alicia Ouellette

In the following viewpoint, Alicia Ouellette argues that cosmetic surgery can be used to eliminate ethnic characteristics to fit a Caucasian standard. Ouellette, a contributor to the Hastings Center Report, *uses an example of the eye-shaping surgery that is performed on many people of Asian descent to illustrate how surgery is used for purely cosmetic purposes and not for any medical or functional reasons. The eye-shaping surgery's sole intention is to make the patient look less Asian and more Western, contends Ouellette. Some people argue that altering the shape of a person's eyes changes her identity, and is done in response to racial stereotypes. This type of cosmetic surgery is especially egregious when performed on a child, who may or may not have a choice in the matter, asserts Ouellette.*

Alicia Ouellette, "Eyes Wide Open: Surgery to Westernize the Eyes of an Asian Child," *Hastings Center Report*, January–February 2009, pp. 15–18. Reproduced by permission.

As you read, consider the following questions:

1. According to the American Society for Aesthetic Plastic Surgery, how many blepharoplasty procedures were performed on Asian Americans in 2005?

2. In addition to the normal risks of surgery, what other complications can result from a blepharoplasty?

3. What are some of the criticisms of eye-shaping surgery for Asians?

The speaker was a proud father. To illustrate his comments about a piece of art that celebrated the wonders of modern medicine (and which he had just donated to a local hospital), he told a story about his adopted Asian daughter. He described her as a beautiful, happy child in whom he took much delight. Her life, he told the audience, had been improved dramatically by the miracle of modern medicine. When she joined her new Caucasian family, her eyes, like those of many people of Asian descent, lacked a fold in the upper eyelid, and that lack was problematic—in his view—because it made her eyes small and sleepy and caused them to shut completely when she smiled. A plastic surgeon himself, he knew she did not need to endure this hardship, so he arranged for her to have surgery to reshape her eyes. The procedure, he explained, was minimally invasive and maximally effective. His beautiful daughter now has big round eyes that stay open and shine even when she smiles.

The case may or may not be unusual in the United States. While surgery to widen the eyes of children, even newborns, is reportedly common in Taiwan, Japan, and Korea, no statistics are available on its use in children in the United States. The Web site of the American Academy of Facial Plastic and Reconstructive Surgery reports that "Asian eye surgery," or blepharoplasty, is the most common procedure elected by Asian Americans, and the American Society for Aesthetic Plastic

Surgery reports that more than 230,000 such procedures were performed in 2005, but since no report breaks that number down by the patient's age and ethnicity or even mentions surgeries performed on children, blepharoplasty may be performed on children only rarely.

On the other hand, no specific legal barriers block the use of plastic surgery on children, and the American Academy of Facial Plastic and Reconstructive Surgery code of ethics says only that "a member must not perform a surgical operation that is not calculated to improve or benefit the patient." A nonscientific but reasonably thorough survey of Web sites advertising Asian eye surgery revealed just one group of physicians that expressly sets a minimum age of eighteen for the surgery, and a search of chat rooms indicates that some families in the United States have obtained the surgery for their daughters. In an article in *Salon* in 2000, Christina Valhouli wrote of families traveling from the United States to Taiwan or Korea to obtain the surgery, but no hard data are available on how often that occurs.

Even if such cases are relatively rare, however, they merit consideration. The intervention is distinctive because its purpose is to shape the child solely for the sake of shaping the child, not to provide a medical or functional benefit. Because the surgery is triggered by a cosmetic preference, it raises stark questions about the limits of parental choice and the failure of the current model of medical decision-making to take into account the rights of the child. In the law's existing paradigm for parental decision-making, eye-shaping is a run-of-the-mill decision requiring deference to parental choice. The case stands as a clear example of the need to reconceptualize the legal role of parents in medical decision-making to better protect children from well-meaning but misguided parents.

The Law of Shaping

Current law affords parents broad, well-recognized rights to shape their children, whether the shaping is figurative (such as cultivating a love of music or reading through early exposure) or literal (such as cultivating a lean body through limited diet and enforced exercise). Indeed, the right of parents to shape their children's lives by deciding where they will live, how they will be educated, and what values they will be taught is so fundamental that it receives constitutional protection. To the extent that the law gives parents the right to shape their children, it treats children "like a special kind of 'property'" over which parents have exclusive control.

Of course, the right of parents to shape their children is not unlimited. Parents cannot use excessive physical violence to teach a lesson. They must feed, clothe, and protect their children. If they neglect those duties or physically abuse their children, they can lose the right to raise them. In such cases, the law recognizes that "the parents are trustees of their children's separate welfare, not owners of their personhood."

When it comes to health care decisions, the law supports a parental prerogative to make choices for children. In virtually all cases, parents are free to choose for their children among reasonable medical alternatives. Indeed, the law presumes that a parent's medical decision for a child is in the child's best interests, and the presumption is difficult to overcome if a provider deems the choice medically reasonable. The parent is thought to be the person best situated to determine the child's best interests, and in making that determination, the parent is free to consider personal and familial values as well as the needs of the individual child.

To be sure, parental power over medical decisions is not unlimited. Theoretically, abuse laws are available to prevent a parent from exposing a child to unnecessary procedures. Child protection laws prohibit parents from acting intentionally to cause or to risk causing physical harm to their children unless the risk is offset by a direct benefit. Cases of medical neglect for failure to treat are not uncommon, but cases in which a parent is found to be abusive for choosing to provide medical care for a child are few and far between. They involve repeated misuse of medical interventions, such as in Munchhausen's by proxy.

The more important limitations on parental choice are procedure- or intervention-specific. In some states, children must be vaccinated regardless of parental choice. In others, parents may not deny children life-sustaining treatment or sterilize a minor without express court approval. Federal law criminalizes female genital cutting, and federal and state laws strictly limit the ability of parents to enroll their children in research protocols. To the extent that the law limits parental choices for children in specific situations, it acknowledges that parents are only trustees of their children's welfare, not owners of their personhoods. Owners may freely destroy their property; trustees are legally bound to protect what they hold in trust. But because the laws limiting parental choice are procedure-specific, not based on a broader conception of the child as person or on a categorical view of parent as trustee, the rule giving priority to parental choice remains the default.

Elective shaping procedures almost always fall within the broad default rule of parental choice. Parents may elect surgery to pin back a child's ears, circumcise a newborn son's penis, repair a cleft palate, or remove a mole from a child's face. The exceptions to the rule are the procedure-specific rules mentioned above: female genital cutting and surgical sterilization of a minor. None applies to eye-shaping surgery.

Thus, unless it could be characterized as an abuse case—which would be difficult given the utter lack of supporting precedent—current law would treat the case of the father who chose to reshape his daughter's eyes no differently from those of a mother who opts to pin back her child's ears, the couple that chooses to circumcise a newborn son, or the father who agrees to hormone treatment to add height to his child. It is a matter of parental choice, limited only by finances and the

Caucasian-Looking Stars

Celebrity plastic surgery Web sites have speculated that J.Lo [Jennifer Lopez] has undergone multiple surgeries to lessen her ethnic features (lip reduction, rhinoplasty to create a more aqualine nose, etc.). . . . And she's not the only megastar who looks like she's had surgery to look more racially ambiguous. Both Beyonce [Knowles] and Halle Berry have smaller, more Caucasian-looking noses than when they began their careers. And let's not even get into Janet Jackson or Lil' Kim.

Faking Good Breeding [blog],
"The Whiteness Makeover," March 8, 2007.

availability of a willing provider. The question the case raises, then, is whether the existing paradigm is adequate.

In the Eye of the Beholder: What Is at Stake?

It is hard to say that the father was not acting in his child's best interest, as he defined it, when he opted for surgery. Nonetheless, the case is troubling. Not only was his child exposed to the actual harm of surgery for purely cosmetic reasons, but she may have been damaged in less tangible but no less important ways.

The literature describes blepharoplasty on the Asian eye as a straightforward and fairly simple procedure. After the patient is sedated and anesthetized, the surgeon makes an incision above the eyelid and removes skin, tissue under the skin, and fat pads. The surgeon then sutures the incision and packs the eye with a light dressing. Once the wound heals, the incision disappears in the newly formed crease. In addition to the usual risks of surgery, eye-shaping surgery poses the risk of hematoma, asymmetry, and drooping. Recovery may be uncomfortable.

Although some women see the surgery as a rite of passage, it is controversial even for adults. Christina Valhouli quoted a twenty-nine-year-old Korean American as saying that she "had the eyelid surgery done her junior year of high school, largely because of nudging from her mother, who had it done as a child in Korea." A young woman on *The Oprah Winfrey Show* explained that eye-shaping surgery "wasn't a vanity thing. It really was this belief that if you looked a little more Western and a little less Asian, it's like having a great degree from a better school. . . . It was something to put in your portfolio." Others condemn the surgery as an attack on ethnic identity. Another woman quoted by Valhouli describes the surgery as "trying to get rid of something that is so distinctly ethnic." Eugenia Kaw argues that "The desire to create more 'open' eyes or 'sharpen' noses is a product of racial ideologies that associate Asian features with negative behavioral or intellectual characteristics like dullness, passivity, or lack of emotion (the proverbial Oriental bookworm)."

Surgeons have become increasingly conscious of the criticism of the surgery and have developed techniques to duplicate naturally occurring Asian double-eyelids, theoretically allowing them to open the eyes without "Westernizing" them.

Despite the controversy, hundreds of thousands of Asian American adults have elected to have eye-shaping surgery for the same reasons the surgeon-father chose it for his daughter. If the father was the decision-maker for the child—the person best situated to decide what is in his child's best interest—and he determined that surgery was in her best interest, then his election of surgery for his daughter was quite appropriate.

The problem with this reasoning, of course, is that the child is, well, a child. She is an individual with full personhood rights, but an incomplete capacity to exercise all those rights. Unlike an adult who chooses to expose herself to the physical risks of surgery, she exercised no choice and was unable to reach and express her own view on the value of the controversial surgery. Her father made choices and imposed them on her.

The same can be said about all medical choices made by parents for children, but two things separate this case from the run-of-the-mill medical case. First, no medical, psychological, or physical impairment triggered the need for a parental decision; the father chose the surgery based on his aesthetic preference. Second, the intervention itself permanently altered a feature that is to some people an integral aspect of identity. These points make a moral difference. Most parental decisions to treat a child medically or surgically are a response to a physical or psychological impairment, illness, or injury in the child. In those cases, some need of the child triggers the decision to intervene, and the parent is the best person to sort through the medically appropriate choices for the child. But when a parent modifies features of a child that have nothing to do with physical impairment but can be integral to identity, and bases that decision on his own needs or aesthetic preferences, he asserts physical control over the child's body in the same way that he might assert control over a piece of property that he can modify to his specifications.

The point can also be put in terms of the child's autonomy. A child has autonomy interests even if she currently lacks the power or capacity to exercise them. While a parent must sometimes act as the child's agent to exercise those autonomy interests, this power is not unbounded. The parent holds the child's right to autonomy in trust. As trustee, the parent must sometimes make choices for the child, but he must also preserve certain choices for the adult the child will become. For example, he cannot choose whom his child will marry, as this choice rightly belongs to her alone when she is grown. The same principle applies to medical decisions. The parent has a duty to preserve for the child the right to make her own decisions about controversial, unnecessary surgery until that child is an adult unless some medical or other necessity triggers the need for an immediate decision. When needs arise, meeting them through an immediate parental decision is more important than preserving the child's ability to make her own decisions in the future. But when intervention is sought to "improve" a child through surgery or medicine for cultural or aesthetic reasons, the impairment to the child's autonomy is hard to justify.

The nature of the surgery makes the case especially troubling. For some people, the shape of the eye is an integral part of ethnicity, a component of identity. A change to it may, therefore, go deeper than the removal of a mole or the pinning of a child's ears. In choosing the surgery, the father took from his daughter the ability to make her own choice about her identity. His exercise of parental autonomy thus limited his daughter's potential autonomy in a critical way; it took away her right to make a decision central to her identity as an adult, a right that is, like others, central to an open future.

In this way, the case is similar to those involving surgical "correction" of ambiguous genitalia, and even female genital cutting. Scholarship about the long-term effects of genital assignment surgery makes a strong case that surgically assigning a gender to a child born with ambiguous genitals may have horrific consequences as the child matures. And female genital cutting—a culture-bound, medically unnecessary ritual—is so harmful to a child's future sexuality that it is banned in all cases, even in those in which physical trauma is minimal. Gender and sexuality are integral components of identity. So, too, is ethnicity. Just as genital surgery and female genital cutting may cause long-term psychological trauma through an insult to identity, so the permanent modification of a child's eye may cause trauma through its insult on identity. At the very least, the long-term consequences of eye-shaping surgery on children are unknown.

The fact that the father was a new adoptive parent makes his decision feel particularly egregious. Perhaps because adoption already involves an exchange, worries about ownership seem closer to the surface. As a result, the adoptive parent seems to have a stronger obligation to accept the child's individuality, especially if the adoption is cross-cultural or cross-racial. But this is a matter of appearances. All parents have the same obligation to accept the child as an individual with separate interests from the parent.

Toward a New Paradigm

The case of eye-opening surgery for an adoptive Asian daughter should open our eyes to the need to reexamine the paradigm that defers to parental choices concerning health care for children when the medical intervention sought addresses the social, cultural, or aesthetic preferences of the parent rather than a medical condition in the child. A paradigm built around the conceptual framework of parent as trustee of the child's welfare would better protect a child from well-meaning but harmful parental decisions than does the current paradigm, with its emphasis on parental choice. The specifics of such a paradigm are beyond the scope of this essay, but certain guiding principles should apply.

First—as with any trustee—a parent's primary duty must be to protect and preserve what is held in trust. Second, the trustee parent must avoid self-dealing—that is, taking advantage of his position as trustee to serve his own interests. Third, the trustee parent may not engage in transactions that involve or create a conflict between his duty to protect the child and his personal interests. As with any trust situation, the trustee's power to exercise his discretion over the trusteeship should be afforded presumptive deference and remain beyond review except to the extent that its exercise is inconsistent with his duties to the child. Those trustee decisions that may constitute an abuse of trust—such as those that suggest self-dealing or that involve a conflict of interest—should be implemented only when reviewed and deemed appropriate by someone other than the trustee.

Applying these principles to medical decisions made by parents for children would maintain the deference given to decisions that are triggered by a physical or psychological need in a child. Decisions to use medicine or surgery to shape a child based on a parent's social, cultural, or aesthetic preferences—especially those that limit the child's ability to make significant choices central to his or her identity—would be treated differently. In such cases, a parent should have the burden of proving that his or her choice for the child will benefit the child in the long run. The responsibility for evaluating such decisions might fall to a neutral third party, the physician, an ethics committee, or a court; but unless someone other than the parent finds convincing evidence that the proposed intervention will address an immediate need of the child's, the intervention should be put off until the child can make her own decision.

> "The increasing number of nonwhites getting cosmetic surgery is helping society accelerate from a crawl to a full-bore sprint toward one truly melted, fusion community."

Cosmetic Surgery Is Moving Toward Multiethnic Beauty Ideals

Anupreeta Das

In the following viewpoint, Anupreeta Das questions whether minorities go under the knife to look more Caucasian. She suggests that as ethnically ambiguous beauties emerge in entertainment and the media, many African American, Asian, and Latino cosmetic-surgery patients want changes that harmonize with their ethnic features. In fact, Das states more surgeons today are specializing in race-specific procedures. This blending and reducing of racial characteristics through cosmetic surgery allow minorities to fit in with beauty standards that are moving away from a Caucasian ideal, she claims. Das is a journalist based in Boston.

Anupreeta Das, "The Search for Beautiful," *Boston Globe*, January 21, 2007. Reproduced by permission of the author.

As you read, consider the following questions:

1. As stated by Das, how do rhinoplasty procedures differ among Caucasians, African Americans, and Asian Americans?

2. Why did Jewish people embrace cosmetic surgery, according to the viewpoint?

3. According to Das, what do critics say about the increase of ethnic models in the fashion industry?

For almost a century, the women who have turned to cosmetic surgery to achieve beauty—or some Hollywood-meets-Madison Avenue version of it—were of all ages, shapes, and sizes but almost always of one hue: white. But now, when there seems to be nothing that a few thousand dollars can't fix, women of color are clamoring in skyrocketing numbers to have their faces and bodies nipped, snipped, lifted, pulled, and tucked. This is a step forward, right? In the land of opportunity, we applaud when barriers break down and more people get to partake in the good life, as it were.

There are many explanations for the new willingness of minorities to go under the knife: their swelling numbers and disposable income, the popularization of cosmetic surgery and its growing acceptance as a normal beauty routine, and its relative affordability. What's significant are the procedures minorities are choosing. More often than not, they're electing to surgically narrow the span of their nostrils and perk up their noses or suture their eyelids to create an extra fold. Or they're sucking out the fat from buttocks and hips that, for their race or ethnicity, are typically plump. It all could lead to one presumption: These women are making themselves look more white—or at least less ethnic.

But perhaps not to the extent some suppose. "People want to keep their ethnic identity," says Dr. Arthur Shektman, a Wellesley-based plastic surgeon. "They want some change, but they don't really want a white nose on a black face." Shektman says not one of his minority patients—they make up about 30 percent of his practice, up from about 5 percent 10 years ago—has said, "I want to look white." He believes this is evidence that the dominant Caucasian-centered idea of blond, blue-eyed beauty is giving way to multiple "ethnic standards of beauty," with the likes of Halle Berry, Jennifer Lopez, and Lucy Liu as poster girls.

"No way" is the answer Tamar Williams of Dorchester gives when asked if her desire to surgically reduce the width of her nose and get a perkier tip was influenced by a Caucasian standard. "Why would I want to look white?" Growing up, the 24-year-old African-American bank teller says, she longed for a nose that wasn't quite so wide or flat or big for her face. "It wasn't that I didn't like it," Williams says. "I just wanted to change it." Hoping to become a model, she thinks the nose job she got in November [2007] will bring her a lifetime of happiness and opportunity. "I was always confident. But now I can show off my nose."

Yet others are less convinced that the centuries-old fixation on Caucasian beauty—from the Mona Lisa to Pamela Anderson—has slackened. "I'm not ready to put to rest the idea that the white ideal has not permeated our psyches," says Janie Ward, a professor of Africana Studies at Simmons College. "It is still shaping our expectations of what is beautiful."

A Peculiar Fusion

Whether or not the surging number of minority patients is influenced by a white standard, one point comes with little doubt: The $12.4 billion-a-year plastic surgery industry is adapting its techniques to meet this demand. The American Academy of Facial Plastic and Reconstructive Surgery (AAFPRS), for example, has in recent months held meetings on subjects ranging from Asian upper-eyelid surgery to so-called ethnic rhinoplasty. The discussion will come to Boston this summer [2007] when the academy will host a five-day event that will include sessions on nose reshaping techniques tailored to racial groups. And increasingly, plastic surgeons are wooing minorities—who make up one-third of the US population—by advertising specializations in race-specific surgeries and using a greater number of nonwhite faces on their Web sites.

It could be that these new patients are not trying to erase the more obvious markers of their ethnic heritage or race, but simply to reduce them. In the process, they're pursuing ethnic and racial ambiguity. Take Williams. With her new smaller nose and long, straight hair, the African-American woman seems to be toying with the idea of ambiguity. And maybe we shouldn't be surprised. The intermingling of ethnicities and races—via marriages, friendships, and other interactions—has created a peculiar fusion in this country. It's the great mishmash where Christmas and Hanukkah and Kwanzaa are celebrated in one long festive spirit, where weddings mix Hindi vows with a chuppah, where California-Vietnamese is a cuisine, where Eminem can be "black" and Beyonce can go blond. And the increasing number of nonwhites getting cosmetic surgery is helping society accelerate from a crawl to a full-bore sprint toward one truly melted, fusion community.

There were 11.5 million cosmetic procedures done in 2005, including surgical ones such as face lifts and rhinoplasties and nonsurgical ones such as Botox shots and collagen injections. One out of every five patients was of African, Asian, or Hispanic descent (separate statistics aren't available for white versus nonwhite Hispanics). According to the American Society for Aesthetic Plastic Surgery, the number of minority patients undergoing cosmetic procedures increased from 300,000 in 1997 to 2 million in 2005. Although the total demand for cosmetic procedures also increased—from 2 million in 1997 to 11.5 million in 2005—the rate of increase for minorities is higher than the overall rate. (Women account for more than nine-tenths of all cosmetic procedures.)

Different ethnic and racial groups favor different procedures. Statistics compiled by the AAFPRS show that in 2005, more than six out of every 10 African-Americans getting cosmetic surgery had nose jobs. Unlike rhinoplasties performed on Caucasians, which may fix a crooked bridge or shave off a hump, doctors say African-American and Asian-American nose reshaping usually leads to narrower nostrils, a higher bridge, and a pointier tip.

For Asian-Americans, eyelid surgery—either the procedure to create an eyelid fold, often giving the eye a more wide-open appearance, or a regular eye lift to reduce signs of aging—is popular. According to the AAFPRS, 50 percent of Asian patients get eyelid surgery. Dr. Min Ahn, a Westborough-based plastic surgeon who performs Asian eyelid surgery, says only about half of the Asian population is born with some semblance of an eyelid crease. "Even if Asians have a preexisting eyelid crease, it is lower and the eyelid is fuller." For those born without the crease, he says, creating the double eyelid is "so much a part of the Asian culture right now." It's probable that this procedure is driving the Asian demand for eyelid surgeries.

Breast augmentation and rhinoplasty top the list of preferred procedures for patients of Hispanic origin, followed by liposuction. Asian-Americans also choose breast implants, while breast reduction—the one procedure eligible for insurance coverage—is the third most preferred choice for African-American women after nose reshaping and liposuction. Doctors say African-American women typically use liposuction to remove excess fat from their buttocks and hips—two areas in which a disproportionate number of women of this race store fat.

The Culture of Self-Improvement

Of course, the assimilative nature of society in general has always demanded a certain degree of conformity and adaptation of every group that landed on American shores. People have adjusted in ways small and large—such as by changing their names and learning new social mores. Elizabeth Haiken, a San Francisco Bay area historian and the author of the 1997 book *Venus Envy: A History of Cosmetic Surgery*, says ethnic minorities may use plastic surgery as a way to fit in to the mainstream, just as another group used it in the early 20th century. "The first group to really embrace cosmetic surgery was the Jews," says Haiken. Her research indicates that during the 1920s, when cosmetic surgery first became popular in the United States, being Jewish was equated with "being ugly and un-American," and the Jewish nose was the first line of attack. Most rhinoplasties therefore sought to reduce its distinct characteristics and bring it more in line with the preferred straighter shape of the Anglo-Saxon nose.

That people would go to such extremes to change their appearance should come as no surprise. "Going back to early 20th-century culture, there is a deep-seated conviction that you are what you look like," Haiken says. "It's not your family, your birth, or your heritage, it's all about you. And your looks and appearance and the way you present yourself will determine who you are." In the initial sizing-up, the face is the fortune. Physical beauty becomes enmeshed with success and happiness.

Plastic surgeons commonly say that minorities today choose surgery for the same reasons as whites—to empower, better, and preserve themselves. "It's the universal desire to maintain youthfulness, and it doesn't change from group to group," says Dr. Frank Fechner, a Worcester-based plastic surgeon.

The culture of self-improvement that surrounds Americans has also made plastic surgery more permissible in recent years. "Making oneself over—one's home, one's car, one's breasts—is now a part of the American life cycle," writes *New York Times* columnist Alex Kuczynski in her 2006 book, *Beauty*

Junkies: Inside Our $15 Billion Obsession With Cosmetic Surgery. "Doctors have sold us on the notion that surgery . . . is merely part of the journey toward enhancement, the beauty outside ultimately reflecting the beauty within." Nothing captures this journey better than the swarm of plastic surgery TV shows such as ABC's *Extreme Makeover*, Fox's *The Swan*, and FX's *Nip/Tuck*. These prime-time televised narratives of desperation and triumph, with the scalpel in the starring role of savior, have also helped make plastic surgery more widely accepted. Through sanitized, pain-free, 60-minute capsules showcasing the transformation of ordinary folks, reality TV has sold people on the notion that the Cinderella story is a purchasable, everyday experience that everyone deserves.

Mei-Ling Hester, a 43-year-old Taiwanese-American hairdresser on Newbury Street, believes in plastic surgery as a routine part of personal upkeep. So when her eyelids started to droop and lose their crease, she rushed to Ahn, the plastic surgeon. He sucked the excess fat out while maintaining, he says, "the Asian characteristic" of her eyelids. Hester also regularly gets Botox injected into her forehead and is considering liposuction. "I feel great inside," she says. With hair tinted a rich brown and eyes without lines or puffiness, her beauty is groomed and serene. "I work out, I eat right, I use good products on my face. It was worth it," she says of her surgery. Although Hester says she pursues plastic surgery for betterment and self-fulfillment, she recognizes her privileged status as someone born with the double eyelids and sharper nose so prized in much of the Asian community. "I just got lucky, because if you look at my sister, she's got a flat nose." Another sister was born without the eyelid crease and had it surgically created, says Hester.

The concept of the double eyelid as beautiful comes from the West. "For many, many years, the standards for beauty have been Western standards that say you have to have a certain shape to the eye, and the eyelid has to have a fold," says

Dr. Ioannis Glavas, a facial plastic surgeon specializing in eyelid surgery, with practices in Cambridge, New York City, and Athens. Sometimes, the demand for bigger eyes can be extreme. Glavas recalls one young Asian-American woman he saw who, in addition to wanting a double eyelid procedure, asked him to snip off some of the bottom lid to expose more of the white. "I had to say no to her," he says.

Glavas says both Asian women and men demand the double eyelid surgery because it is a way of looking less different by reducing an obvious ethnic feature. Presumably, Asian patients aren't aiming to look white by getting double eyelids (after all, African-Americans and other minorities have double eyelids), but the goal is social and cultural assimilation, or identification with some dominant aesthetic standard.

Across-the-Board Appeal

In recent years, the dominant aesthetic standard in American society has moved away from the blond, blue-eyed Caucasian woman to a more ethnically ambiguous type. Glossy magazines are devoting more pages to this melting-pot aesthetic, designed (like the new Barbies) for across-the-board appeal. Today's beautiful woman comes in many colors, from ivory to cappuccino to ebony. Her hair can be dark and kinky, and she might even show off a decidedly curvy derriere—a feature that has actually started to prompt some white women to get gluteal augmentation, or butt implants.

However, critics say these are superficial changes to what is essentially a Caucasian-inspired ideal—the big-eyed, narrow-nosed, pillow-lipped, large-breasted, boyishly thin apparition. "There has been a subtle change in the kind of models you see in Victoria's Secret catalogs or *Vogue*," says Dr. Fred Stucker, the head of facial plastic surgery at Louisiana State University, Shreveport. But "they take the black girl who has the high cheekbones, narrow nose, and pouty lips." It's not uncommon, he says, to find "a white face with dark skin."

Cultural Standards Remain Diverse

Bahman Teimourian of Bethesda, a clinical professor of plastic surgery at Georgetown University School of Medicine, said it behooves surgeons of all races to be knowledgeable about cultural standards.

A chin that might be considered weak by traditional American standards and a candidate for plastic surgery, Teimourian said, is seen as beautiful among people from the Middle East, where a small chin is regarded as a desirable sign of femininity.

Recently Teimourian said he repaired the nose of an African American patient who was unhappy with the "very Caucasian nose" a previous surgeon had given her. Teimourian said he removed some cartilage from behind the woman's ear to reshape her nose to better fit her features.

Sandra G. Boodman,
"Cosmetic Surgery Goes Ethnic,"
The Washington Post, *May 29, 2007.*

Going by the recent surge of minorities demanding plastic surgery, it is plausible that this attempt by canny marketers and media types to promote a darker-skinned but still relatively uniform ideal is working. After all, they are simply following the money. According to the University of Georgia's Selig Center for Economic Growth, which compiles an annual report on the "multicultural economy" in the United States, minorities had a combined buying power of several trillion dollars in 2006. In 2007, the disposable income of Hispanics is expected to rise to $863 billion, while African-Americans will collectively have $847 billion to spend. By 2010, Asians are expected to have buying power totaling $579 billion. And all of these groups are showing a greater willingness to spend it on themselves and the things they covet, including cosmetic surgery.

Katie Marcial represents exactly this kind of person. The 50-year-old African-American is newly single, holds a well-paying job in Boston, and has no qualms about spending between $10,000 and $20,000 on a tummy tuck and breast surgery. "I'm doing this mainly because I'm economically able to do so," says Marcial, a Dorchester resident whose clear skin and youthful attire belie her age. With her three children all grown, her money is hers to spend. "I can indulge in a little vanity," she says. Marcial says she chose a young, Asian-American doctor to perform her surgery because "I thought she would know the latest techniques and be sensitive to ethnic skin."

Historically, plastic surgery has been tailored to Caucasian women. Glavas says that in medical texts, the measurements of symmetry and balance—two widely recognized preconditions of beauty—were made with Caucasian faces in mind. Such practices led to a general sense among minorities that plastic surgery was for whites and kept them away from tinkering with their faces and bodies. But even as the industry now adapts to its new customers, plastic surgeons are divided over whether surgical specialization in various ethnicities and races necessarily caters better to the needs of minority patients. Dr. Julius Few, a plastic surgeon at Northwestern University's Feinberg School of Medicine, hails the fact that plastic surgeons are customizing their procedures to focus on minorities, "so it's not just the one-size-fits-all mentality of saying, well, if somebody's coming in, regardless, they're going to look Northern European coming out." He even sees "a sort of subspecialty" emerging in various ethnic procedures. Meanwhile, Dr. Jeffrey Spiegel, who is chief of facial plastic and reconstructive surgery at Boston University Medical Center and has a large number of nonwhite patients, is skeptical of the notion of specialization in ethnic and racial cosmetic surgery. "It strikes me more as a marketing tool than a real specialization," he says.

In 1991, Michael Jackson crooned "It don't matter if you're black or white." Jackson's message about transcending race may have won singalong supporters, but his plastic surgeries did not. His repeated nose jobs and lightened skin color (he has maintained he is not bleaching but is using makeup to cover up the signs of vitiligo, a skin condition) were perceived by minorities—especially African-Americans—as an attempt to look white. Doctors say that "Don't make me look like Michael Jackson" is a popular refrain among patients. "People were put off by dramatic surgeries and preferred subtle changes," says Shektman, the Wellesley-based plastic surgeon.

The New Melting-Pot Aesthetic

Choices have expanded since then. Minorities can now hold themselves up against more ethnically and racially ambiguous role models that may still trace their roots to the once-dominant Caucasian standard but are becoming more composite and blended. "The concept of ideal beauty is moving toward a mix of ethnic features," says plastic surgeon Ahn, a Korean-American who is married to a Caucasian. "And I think it's better."

The push toward ethnic and racial ambiguity should perhaps be expected, because the cultural churn in American society is producing it anyway. Sure, promoting ambiguous beauty is a strategic move on the part of marketing gurus to cover their bases and appeal to all groups. But it's also a reflection of reality. Not only are minorities expected to make up about half the American population by 2050, but the number of racially mixed people is increasing tremendously. The number of mixed-race children has been growing enough since the 1970s that in 2000 the Census Bureau created a new section in which respondents could self-identify their race;

nearly 7 million people (2.4 percent of the population) identified themselves as belonging to more than one race.

For minorities, this new melting-pot beauty aesthetic—perhaps the only kind of aesthetic standard that befits a multiethnic and multicultural society—is an achievable and justifiable goal. Increasingly, advertisements use models whose blue eyes and dreadlocked hair or almond-shaped eyes and strong cheekbones leave you wondering about their ethnic origins. The ambiguous model might have been dreamed up on a computer or picked from the street. But advertisers value her because she is a blended product—someone everyone can identify with because she cannot be immediately defined by race or ethnicity. By surgically blending or erasing the most telling ethnic or racial characteristics, cosmetic surgery makes ambiguity possible and allows people of various ethnicities and races to fit in. For the Jewish community in the 1920s, fitting in may have had to do with imitating a Caucasian beauty ideal. For minorities today, it's a melting-pot beauty ideal that is uniquely American. How appropriate this ambiguity is, in a culture that expects conformity even as it celebrates diversity.

Periodical Bibliography

The following articles have been selected to supplement the diverse views presented in this chapter.

Asia Pacific Post	"Asian Eyes Are In as Beauty Ideals Shift," May 7, 2008.
Dan Bilefsky	"If Plastic Surgery Won't Convince You, What Will?" *New York Times*, May 24, 2009.
Robert Burton	"How Looks Can Kill," *Salon*, January 31, 2008.
Ruth Charney	"The Many Faces of Plastic Surgery," *wowOwow*, June 17, 2009.
Jennifer Cognard-Black	"Extreme Makeover: Feminist Edition," *Ms.*, Summer 2007.
Carlin Flora	"The Beguiling Truth About Beauty: Not a Knockout?" *Psychology Today*, May–June 2006.
Dean Kaufman	"Do You Think You're Beautiful?" *O, The Oprah Magazine*, April 2006.
Caomhan Keane and Leah Sullivan	"In Defense of Plastic Surgery," *The Dubliner*, February 19, 2008.
Wendy McElroy	"In Defense of Beauty Pageants," LewRockwell.com, November 19, 2004.
Matthew Shulman	"Teens Getting Plastic Surgery: Be Cautious," *U.S. News and World Report*, July 1, 2008.

OPPOSING
VIEWPOINTS®
SERIES

CHAPTER 4

What Are the Effects of the Beauty and Fashion Industries?

Chapter Preface

In August 2008, a L'Oréal's print advertisement for hair color featuring Beyoncé more than raised a few eyebrows. Being that she was born of African American and Creole descent, the pop star's caramel complexion seemed suspiciously pale, her blond, pin-straight locks adding to the racial ambiguity of her appearance. Critics swiftly accused the French beauty corporation of whitewashing Beyoncé's skin tone. The *New York Post* ran a story called "Beyoncé the Pale," claiming that digital lightening made "the world-famous singer virtually unrecognizable."[1] TMZ conducted an online poll asking its readers if the ad was "a slap to Blacks,"[2] and 58 percent agreed. Said one commentator on the Web site, "Shame on L'Oréal for doing this. . . . If it was uneven skin tone then they just as easily could have made her a tone darker. But they did not do that. They made her white."[3] Nonetheless, in a statement released to the Associated Press, L'Oréal denied the allegation: "We highly value our relationship with Ms. Knowles. It is categorically untrue that L'Oréal Paris altered Ms. Knowles' features or skin tone in the campaign for Feria hair color."[4]

From the pre-digital age of airbrushing to the point-and-click wizardry of Photoshop, cosmetics advertising and fashion magazines have been assailed for conditioning the public with unrealistic images of beauty. In response, celebrities from actress Keira Knightly to socialite Kim Kardashian have recently come forward to address the differences between their real bodies and their idealized selves seen in glossy campaigns and pictorials. Taking the concept further, French *Elle* published a series of covers for its April 2009 edition titled "Stars Sans Fards [Makeup]" that lived up to its claim—eight female stars without makeup or retouching. In the following chapter, the authors examine how the beauty industry affects the everyday lives of consumers.

Notes

1. David K. Li, *New York Post*, August 7, 2008.
2. TMZ, August 6, 2008.
3. TMZ, August 6, 2008.
4. Associated Press, August 7, 2008.

> *"The reshaped bodies, the smoothed-out wrinkles, 'all that is there to alter your mind, to alter your conception of what physical beauty is.'"*

The Beauty Industry Promotes Unrealistic Beauty Standards

Stacy Malkan

Stacy Malkan is cofounder of the Campaign for Safe Cosmetics and author of Not Just a Pretty Face: The Ugly Side of the Beauty Industry. *In the following viewpoint excerpted from* Not Just a Pretty Face, *she claims that the beauty industry bombards women with cosmetic and fashion advertisements that are airbrushed and retouched to false perfection. In pursuit of these artificial, Western beauty standards, many women use products with ingredients that are dangerous to human health, Malkan alleges. According to the author, skin treatments available in Asia that promise fairer complexions often contain toxic heavy metals and carcinogens, and hair relaxers and other styling products expose African American women to poisonous chemicals and cancer-causing agents.*

As you read, consider the following questions:

1. What is Anne Larracas's opinion of skin-lightening products in the Philippines?

2. According to the viewpoint, in what ways was a photo of Halle Berry altered?

3. How, in the author's view, has the Caucasian beauty ideal affected African American women?

> *For centuries, Japanese women have known a secret, the secret of beautiful skin. Prepare to discover the secret of SK-II for yourself. Many years ago, a Japanese monk noticed that the workers in a sake brewery had extraordinarily smooth hands. He was determined to discover why. After many experiments, he discovered a liquid that seemed to defy aging . . .*
>
> —*Advertisement for the premium brand of SK-II skin care products*

More recently, Chinese authorities made a discovery of their own about SK-II products: the high-end skin whitening cream and powders contained the toxic heavy metals chromium and neodymium. "Hundreds of angry Chinese women have taken to the streets of Shanghai demanding refunds for US-Japanese cosmetics after authorities detected banned chemicals in some of the products," reported the *Agence France Presse* in September 2006. "Security guards were called in Thursday to control a crowd of about 300 people, infuriated over being made to wait over promised refunds for the affected SK-II cosmetics owned by US consumer products giant Procter and Gamble."

P&G temporarily suspended sales of the SK-II line and closed sales counters across China after "security incidents" broke out between employees and customers and a furious mob smashed a glass door at the company's Shanghai branch. Thousands of consumers demanded refunds of the elite brand that sells for more than $100 a bottle. It was a dramatic interruption in the otherwise relatively smooth and recent entry of multinational cosmetics corporations into the world's largest market.

The heavy metals chromium and neodymium, which can cause eczema and allergic dermatitis, are banned from cosmetics in China, although there are few other restrictions on personal care products. Procter & Gamble said the metals exist naturally, were not intentionally added to SK-II products and were safe at the low levels found in the products. In October, Chinese authorities announced the trace levels of metals would not harm consumers with normal use of the products, and by December SK-II products were slowly making their way back onto stores shelves.

Back at P&G company headquarters in the US, the episode presented no apparent difficulties. "The interruption is not expected to affect P&G's financial results," reported the *Cincinnati Enquirer*, in the city where the company's headquarters are based. "Sales in mainland China are only about 7% of global SK-II sales, and Procter said it removed SK-II from shelves simply to remove its products from the controversy until they were declared safe. China is P&G's fastest-growing market, with beauty-care products making up the bulk of the company's more than $2 billion in sales there."

White Hot

Skin whitening is all the rage in Asian countries like the Philippines, where the most popular actresses are light skinned, thin-nosed and appear in the ads for products that promise pale skin. "We're bombarded with advertisements like that every day. Every beauty product in the Philippines has a lightening aspect. Even lipstick promises to make dark upper lips more pink," said Anne Larracas from Quezon City near Manila.

Products in the category called "skin fading/skin lighteners" are among the most toxic cosmetics in the *Skin Deep* database [a database that lists the ingredients and safety of cosmetics and personal-care products]. Many contain hydroquinone, which works as a skin lightener by decreasing the production of melanin pigments in the skin. The chemical—a confirmed animal carcinogen that is toxic to the skin, brain, immune system and reproductive system—is banned in the European Union but allowed in products sold in the US in concentrations of up to 2%. The US Cosmetic Ingredient Review panel warns the chemical is unsafe for use in products left on the skin, but the recommendation is sometimes ignored. Physicians Complex Skin Bleaching Cream with 2% hydroquinone, for example, advises consumers to "Apply to clean skin twice daily. Desired results are achieved with consistent use of this product." The product, made by CosMed, contains a dozen problematic ingredients, including three chemicals with potential to increase skin cancer risk by intensifying UV exposures in deep skin layers. "Application of Physicians Complex sunblock SPF #30 is mandatory on a daily basis," advises the package.

In the Philippines, where there are no regulated limits, some products, such as the popular Maxi Peel by Splash Corporation, contain 4% hydroquinone. Anne Larracas has friends who use such products, and she said the effects are startling. "When you first use it, as fast as three days, the skin starts to peel and it gets really red. Then the skin gets taut, you can see the veins because it peels too much, and the peeling doesn't stop. The skin gets lighter and lighter and thinner and thinner. Then the face starts to get light and white, but the neck is still dark, so it looks like there is a permanent foundation." Many women don't know they are supposed to also use sunscreen, Anne said. "It's so sad. I don't know why girls would like to whiten their skin."

According to dermatologists, skin color is genetic and no chemical can permanently lighten skin—although hydroquinone can produce temporary whitening effects, as can the heavy metals chromium and mercury, both of which have been detected in skin whitening creams sold in Asia. After the SK-II incident in China, media organizations in Hong Kong tested a range of skin whitening creams and reportedly found chromium in products made by Clinique, Estée Lauder, Christian Dior, Max Factor, Lancôme and Shiseido. Mercury has also been detected in several products made in China and Taiwan. When a patient turned up in his office with mercury poisoning, Dr. Christopher Lam, chair at the department of chemical pathology at Hong Kong's Prince of Wales Hospital, examined her skin whitening cream and found mercury levels 65,000 times higher than amounts allowed in the US. Follow-up product tests conducted by Lam found mercury in eight of 38 skin whitening creams made in China and Taiwan. Some of the products were labeled "mercury free."

Nevertheless, the "thriving *bihaku* (white beauty) boom remains one of the most significant driving forces for overall growth as manufacturers cater to the Asian preference for a fair complexion," reported *Euromonitor*. "According to leading industrial sources, up to 60% of Japanese women use skin whitening products in their daily regime, presenting manufacturers with a strong opportunity for continued growth." The major players have sought to maximize sales by offering "complete skin whitening regimes, comprising not only of moisturizers, but also cleansers, toners, day and night nourishers and even facial cleansing wipes."

Sales are particularly promising in China, which has recorded double digit increases in recent years. The country is now the second largest market by volume for Procter & Gamble, and will someday be first if Daniela Riccardi, president of P&G Greater China, has her way. "Maybe it will take 10 years, but my staff, my company and I are very clear that it will eventually happen," the P&G executive told the *China Daily*. "Now our strategies are designed to touch as many customers in China as possible, step by step," Riccardi said. "Our future objective is to try to reach towns and villages where there are hundreds of millions of people."

Not everyone is thrilled with the market potential. "I'm so pissed about this whitening stuff. It's everywhere," said Anne Larracas from the Philippines. "Every actress we have is light skinned, so when you're a *monena* like me, dark skinned, you have to use whitening products to become famous." Her cousin, a plastic surgeon, keeps teasing her to get a nose job. "The beauty stuff is symbolic of how we've been brainwashed about Western culture. It's the best thing to look Caucasian and blonde, with pretty light skin. And it's not just about beauty products, it's about clothes, iPods, books, TV shows, everything," Anne said. "What needs to happen is that we have to reconnect with who we really are."

Mirror, Mirror on the Wall

Ken Harris admits to feeling a bit guilty about what he does for a living. As a "digital photo retoucher," he airbrushes fashion photos of the glamorous models who broadcast idealized images of beauty around the world. We know, of course, about the airbrushing. Still, it's surprising to see Harris in action in Jesse Epstein's award-winning documentary film *Wet Dreams and False Images*. In the film, Harris demonstrated how he changes skin color, reshapes body parts and shaves pounds off models. "Almost always the first thing I'll do is fix the nose," Harris explained, zipping the computer mouse over a photo. "Every picture has been worked on some 20 or 30 rounds going back and forth between the retouchers and the client and the agency. They're perfected to death," he said. "I don't see these photographs as being authentic or real. I see them as being mechanical and inhuman."

Digital retoucher Dominic Demasi demonstrated in the film how he reworked a photo of actress Halle Berry to remove pockmarks, change her skin tone to match her makeup and even shave down her knuckles to make them "seem less obtrusive." Product manufacturers are "not going to keep something that looks flawed or natural. They're not concerned with natural. They're concerned with selling their product," Demasi explained. "If it looks like it hasn't been touched at all, I've been successful."

The reshaped bodies, the smoothed-out wrinkles, "all that is there to alter your mind, to alter your conception of what physical beauty is . . . and what the means of attaining it are," Harris said. "In that the central point of retouching is to enforce an unrealizable standard of beauty, I suspect of myself some sort of covert obscure misogyny, because I'm really screwing with people's sense of identity and self-worth by doing this." But, he said, he gets paid really well.

The Straight Story

Felicia Eaves was eight when she started with the hair relaxers. Like many African-American girls, her hair was thick and tangled easily, causing many frustrating sessions under the brush. So twice weekly she used hair relaxer and styling aides—pomade or hair grease, as Felicia calls it, which kept her hair from drying out.

Of all the products in *Skin Deep*, those that change the shape and color of hair, such as relaxers, perms and dyes—along with nail products and skin lighteners—have the most toxic ingredients. The conditioners marketed to African-American women can also be problematic. "Instantly repair dry and damaged hair" is a typical marketing claim on hair products containing placenta, the nourishing fetal organ expelled after birth. Placenta products supposedly make hair stronger and more manageable, but they can also contain estrogenic hormones that are linked to early puberty and breast cancer. Some scientists believe that early and lifelong exposure to hormone-containing personal care products may be partly to blame for the high rates of breast cancer in young African-American women.

A Narrowing of the Definition of Beauty

The last fifty years have witnessed an interesting paradox. Beauty—as an idea and an ideal—has moved away from being the exclusive province of the Hollywood dream factory, of fashion models and the young bride, to become an essential attribute to which women of all ages need to pay heed. But at the same time that women of all ages and classes want to claim beauty for themselves, there has been an insidious narrowing of the beauty aesthetic to a limited physical type—thin, tall—which inevitably excludes millions and millions of women. The conjunction between democratizing the *idea* of beauty and the limiting of what constitutes the *ideal* of beauty has caused considerable anguish to women—young to old—who strive to find in themselves the means to meet those aesthetic values which have come to make up what we regard as beautiful.

Susie Orbach, "The Real Truth About Beauty:
A Global Report," September 2004.

It's not just the type of products used by African-American women that raises concern, but also the frequency of use. As Felicia Eaves, an organizer for Women's Voices for the Earth, explained, "We use more beauty products than other women, way more." According to market surveys, African-American women are more likely to take bubble baths, get facials and manicures, use scented products, wear lipstick and use bath additives than women of other ethnic groups. Nine out of ten African-American women use health and beauty products to express their individuality, compared to just over half of general-market women. Though they comprise just 12% of the US population, African-American women account for 21% of all hair care expenditures. Part of the reason, Felicia believes, is a special love affair with beauty products that stems from African heritage. The Egyptians were the first to discover and use cosmetics for the purposes of adornment some 6,000 years ago, and the bath ritual has always been an important part of African culture. "So I would say that we are subconsciously remembering what it was like to be in the motherland," said Felicia.

But another part of it, according to Felicia, is "the whole legacy of racism, the feeling that you need to look a certain way to be accepted in this society. The Eurocentric ideal of beauty in this country has really done a psychological job on African Americans. Every actress has a weave, even Oprah. Nobody is wearing their natural hair anymore." Traditional locks and afros are referred to as "extreme hair styles" in the popular culture, and young girls get the clear message about what's acceptable. Felicia has heard of girls as young as five getting weaves or extensions—these can be done naturally, but some involve glues and require acetone- or formaldehyde-based removers to get them off.

Felicia takes it back to "the whole crazy reason women do all this stuff to our bodies in the first place, because of a lack of self-esteem and a need to feel accepted. And it's not just Black women, it's all women." But there's a special pressure on Black women. "Throughout the history of slavery, Black women and men were used as a commodity, and because our look was so different, it was a point to ostracize us. There is this pressure that you have to look a certain way to be accepted. The way I look is still not quite as accepted as the way a White woman looks," Felicia said. "So part of it is about wanting to project a nice-looking image, but it also harkens back to how we've been perceived in this country, as different and other. We tend to want to be very careful about the way we're perceived with looks and hygiene."

In her view, women should be able to do whatever they want for a beauty routine without having to worry about toxic chemicals. "I like wearing makeup; I do get a lift from it. I like trying new colors and matching them with my outfits," Felicia said. "Women should be able to get that lift, but not at the expense of their health. The onus is on the manufacturers to make products that are safe."

Paint Me Poison

As dark-skinned women dreamed of "white beauty," I was booking appointments at the tanning beds and lying for hours on end under the sun. The mineral oils and suntan lotions that promised bronze beauty littered my high school vanity table along with dozens of jars, tubes and wands that covered up my anxieties. For me it was all about the Christie Brinkley fantasy—her flawless skin, that perfect nose! I studied the contours of the supermodel's face, scrutinized my profile, agonized; filled my little makeup bag with the tempting tropical hues that offered up the easy, breezy Cover Girl dream.

Applying new knowledge to old habits, I take a trip back in time to see what secrets I can discover about my frequent forays to the Osco Drug aisle of hope. I typed my teen beauty routine into the *Skin Deep* database. The five shower products, liquid foundation, Clean Pressed Powder and Cheekers Blush; the Perfect Blend Eye Pencil, Expert Wear Shadows and Marathon Mascara, topped off with the daily cloud of Aqua Net Extra Super Hold. I counted 19 products in all—230 chemicals, according to *Skin Deep*, most of them applied to my body before I even left the house to catch the bus to Lynn Classical High. That's well above the average person's estimated daily exposure to cosmetic chemicals. Well, as I said, it was an obsession.

The first thing I notice is: so much for truth in advertising. Healing Garden Mintherapy Moisturizing Body Lotion by Coty Inc. gets the highest toxicity score of all the products on my list—a 4.1 (5 is the highest). Suave Lavender "Naturals" Shampoo and Conditioner by Unilever have 17 problematic ingredients between them. *Skin Deep* tells me: 81 of the chemical ingredients in my former daily routine raise health concerns. Some highlights:

- 22 daily doses of parabens, along with four other suspected hormone-disrupting chemicals.

- 17 hits of chemicals with limited or mixed evidence of carcinogenicity. One ingredient, petroleum distillates in my Cover Girl Marathon Waterproof Mascara, is banned in the European Union.

- 17 applications of penetration enhancers, which can draw the other chemicals more deeply into my body.

- 15 doses of chemicals that persist in the body or accumulate up the food chain.

- 15 products with fragrance—an unspecified mix of chemicals likely to contain phthalates and allergens.

- Less than half the ingredients in my products have been assessed for safety.

My head is spinning. I feel like Alice who fell down the rabbit hole. Down, down, down, until, thump, she goes into a long dark hallway with big keys and tiny locks. What does it all really mean? What does it mean, for instance, that the triethanolamine (or TEA) in my Ban de Soleil sunscreen, Healing Garden body lotion and Cover Girl "clean liquid" makeup has "limited evidence of carcinogenicity"? I delve deeper in the database and find that the chemical (spelled 32 different ways on product labels) forms carcinogenic nitrosamine compounds if mixed with other ingredients that act as nitrosating agents. It is also a skin sensitizer and possibly toxic to the lungs and brain. . . .

So what's young Alice to do? As the landscape tilts and twirls, a picture comes clear: it is exactly the complicating factors of it—the dozens of toxic chemicals, combined into mixtures that have never been assessed for safety—that are the truest truth of all. Nobody can tell me what impact these daily chemical cocktails had on my body. Now, as the Lewis Carroll story goes, wise young Alice already knew to check the bottle to see if it was marked "poison"—"for she had read several nice little stories about children who had got burnt, and eaten up by wild beasts, and other unpleasant things, all because they *would* not remember the simple rules their friends had taught them: such as, that a red-hot poker will burn you if you hold it too long and that, if you cut your finger very deeply with a knife, it usually bleeds; and she had never forgotten that, if you drink much from a bottle marked 'poison,' it is almost certain to disagree with you, sooner or later." But, of course, none of the 19 bottles and tubes on my vanity table carried such a warning.

> *"These days, the general public and the fashion industry seem to have very different ideas about what makes a woman beautiful."*

The Beauty Industry No Longer Embraces the Unrealistic Beauty Standards of Models

Jessica B. Matlin

In the following viewpoint, Jessica B. Matlin claims that models have fallen out of favor with the beauty and cosmetics industries. The author insists that movie and television actresses have taken models' places in makeup and skin-care advertisements because of their attainable, even "down-home" appeal. Moreover, she claims that clothing designers currently seek girls who are unconventional looking, with exaggerated, strong features, further reflecting the different ideas of beauty held in the fashion industry and general public. The author is a beauty writer.

As you read, consider the following questions:

1. How does Matlin describe the current top models?

2. What type of looks are the "kiss of death" in high fashion, as stated by Matlin?

3. According to the author, what is the problem with today's fashion models?

At a dusty gas station in the middle of nowhere, two little boys gawk at a glistening, sweaty vision of Cindy Crawford in all her long-limbed, beauty-marked splendor as she downs a condensation-beaded can of Pepsi.

"Beeeaaauuuuutttiiffuulll . . ." says one Little Rascals look-alike to the other, and audiences watching that 1991 television ad couldn't help but agree.

The commercial is now considered a classic, perhaps because it couldn't be made today. Replace Crawford with one of the fashion world's current top models—Gemma Ward, Julia Stegner, Jessica Stam—and most TV viewers would be left scratching their heads in confusion, as cold as the aforementioned Pepsi. While a decade and a half ago it was possible for a model to simultaneously hawk haute couture and soda pop—and pose for cheesy dorm-room posters signed "Love Always, Cindy"—now even the most successful mannequins are seldom seen beyond the pages of heavy-stock glossies. These days, the general public and the fashion industry seem to have very different ideas about what makes a woman beautiful. And nowhere is that more apparent than in the cosmetics word, where models seem to be falling further and further out of favor. Now even B-list actresses have a better chance of scoring the lucrative fragrance and makeup contracts that used to be a model's ticket to the good life.

"Tunes have changed!" pronounces Aerin Lauder, Estee Lauder's vice president of global advertising, who recently signed thespian Gwyneth Paltrow as the face of the brand's Pleasures perfume. (Professional looker Carolyn Murphy remains Estee Lauder's lead face in skincare and makeup.)

Models Are Disposable

"One of the interesting things about these models today is that they get used and spit out so quickly," says Magali Amadei, a model who has been open about her recovery from bulimia. "The era of the supermodel is over, so girls working today don't have the earning power. These girls come into the business young, and they are disposable. On top of that, people often talk about your appearance in front of you, as if you can't hear them."

Such pressures can be the most intense on girls who walk the runway, a job that possesses a strange, Catch-22 quality. Models must not distract from the clothes, and yet their chance to succeed is to stand out. If she gets noticed, a model can grab the big prize—a major ad campaign. These contracts offer financial security and celebrity, which translates to a modicum of power, although nothing compared with the days when models rather than celebrities commanded the covers of fashion magazines.

Emily Nussbaum,
The Incredibly Shrinking Model,"
New York, *February 26, 2007.*

"People are yearning for an escape. They like to go to the movies and watch their favorite stars. It's the right time to have a celebrity."

Once the Territory of the Glamazons

It's a trend that can be seen across the beauty industry. Revlon, once the territory of glamazons like Cindy and Claudia [Schiffer], now has a roster of spokeswomen that reads more like the guest list of a Golden Globes after-party, a hodgepodge of bona fide A-listers (Susan Sarandon and Julianne Moore) and rising actresses (Kate Bosworth and Eva Mendes). Scarlett Johansson, fresh off her appearance in Calvin Klein's Eternity Moment ads (Christy Turlington Burns had been the Eternity girl for 18 years), was recently named one of the faces of L'Oreal Paris, along with Penelope Cruz. And Ashley Judd's cozy contract with American Beauty was ultimately sealed by her "down-home" appeal, says president Jane Hudis. "The era of the supermodel is over," says Hudis. "Women want something deeper."

While eerily fragile, childlike girls known as "doll faces" are all the rage on the catwalk—think Heather Marks, Lisa Cant, Lily Cole, and the ubiquitous Gemma Ward—MAC cosmetics, which once ran in lockstep with the runways, is taking things in the opposite direction. Its "girl" of the moment this spring? Sixty-two-year-old Catherine Deneuve. "I think models portray a kind of idealized beauty that for the ordinary woman is not attainable," says James Gager, MAC's senior vice president of creative. "Instead, we're paying homage to a more mature, beautiful woman." Gager makes plain that aspiration is still a key concert in the marketing of makeup—consumers, of course, are still more motivated to buy a lipstick that they associate with a beautiful woman. But, he insists, "I think the public is ready to see a less idealized version of what they're supposed to look like."

According to Paul Rowland, owner of Supreme Management, which represents such top models as Anna Barsukova and [the late] Heather Bratton, there are sociological forces driving the cosmetics giants away from catwalk muses. "It's a reflection of the social environment," he says. "There is so much uncertainty in the world that people are gravitating to something that's more conventional."

And what's hot among fashion aesthetes is anything but conventional beauty. On the runway, straightforward, Barbie-doll looks are currently the kiss of death. It's acceptable for a major model to resemble a Kewpie (Gemma), a wood nymph (Natalia) or an almond-eyed feline (Daria), but any likeness to Christie Brinkley is strictly verboten. "[Designers] want 'strong girls.' That is the operative word," says Michelle Lee of fashion PR [public relations] powerhouse KCD, which casts shows for Chloe, Gucci and Marc by Marc Jacobs. "There's been a shift in the trend."

A Wider Customer Base

Of course, the high-fashion world, with its small, elite and highly sophisticated audience, can get away with casting such rarefied cream. A woman with the confidence and where-withal to rock a pair of $2,000 Balenciaga pants will likely not be put off by a model who looks as if she should be onstage at CBGB. The beauty industry, however, has to appeal to a much wider customer base, and even the modeling agents who represent today's top mannequins have to admit that the new girls lack broad appeal. "The general public isn't able to relate to them," says Marilyn Gauthier, president of the Marilyn agency, which counts Caroline Trentini and Lily Donaldson as clients.

So what does this mean for the future of the so-called spokesmodel? Will the cosmetics industry give catwalkers the kiss-off for good? Gauthier, for one, doesn't think so. She firmly believes—perhaps because her livelihood largely depends on it—[that] the everywoman trawling the aisles of CVS for blush and foundation will eventually come around to fashion's current crop of exotics. "The public will see that the special girls become stars. I've seen it happen many times," she says with confidence.

There are some signs that she's right. Lancome, previously promoted by big-screen types like Uma Thurman, Juliette Binoche, and Isabella Rossellini, just hired Daria to be the new face of the brand. "There needs to be reality, but there needs to be fantasy too," says Odile Roujol, Lancome's head of worldwide marketing. At CoverGirl, a company whose moniker is, after all, synonymous with "supermodel," what's going on might hint at the next trend on the horizon. The label, which counts among its current faces Queen Latifah and Molly Sims, recently decided to add a big-name model to its roster. CoverGirl's choice: not Gemma or Heather but, believe it or not, Christie Brinkley.

> "Cosmeceuticals combine the best of both worlds: wellness and beauty, ancient traditions and new science."

Many Cosmeceuticals Are Effective

Heather Granato

In the following viewpoint, Heather Granato claims that "cosmeceuticals" are scientifically proven to promote both wellness and beauty. Neither a drug nor cosmetic, cosmeceuticals can be defined as topical or oral supplements that target skin health. The author insists that natural ingredients with long-touted benefits, such as antioxidants, are incorporated in these products. Therefore, Granato states that they slow the skin's aging processes and diminish lines and wrinkles while protecting from further damage, evidenced by published studies and research. Granato is a group editor at Virgo Publishing, which publishes trade magazines, fact books, and directories in different industries.

As you read, consider the following questions:

1. What ancient examples does Granato provide of skin and personal care?

Heather Granato, "Cosmeceuticals: At the Intersection of Nutrition and Beauty," *Natural Products Insider*, June 4, 2007. Reproduced by permission.

2. What factors are driving the cosmeceuticals market, according to the author?

3. As stated in the viewpoint, how can young, firm skin be achieved?

Throughout history, men and women have sought to use the medicinal power of natural compounds to increase their health, enhance their looks, and fight off aging. The Egyptians used aromatic essences and resins in religious ceremonies and embalming, as well as for cosmetic purposes. Cleopatra, for one, was renowned for her baths of camels' milk and honey—the milk providing a moisturizing, exfoliating, and whitening effect. Across the desert and the Arabian Sea, the Vaidyas in India were practicing integrated holistic health as Ayurveda, incorporating botanicals, oils, and massage into whole body support; and there are countless other examples across the continents. But in "modern society," consumers moved away from traditional practices and products to embrace the promises of futuristic technology. Fortunately, today there is a melding of traditional knowledge and scientific advancement in the world of "cosmeceuticals."

This term, coined in the 1960s by [cosmetic science expert] Raymond Reed and popularized by Albert M. Kligman, a dermatological researcher, has no official or regulatory definition. In fact, the Food and Drug Administration (FDA) does not recognize the category *cosmeceutical*—in its mind, products can be drugs, cosmetics, or a combination of both, often defined by product claims or consumer perception. "Cosmeceutical products promote not only external beauty, but overall whole health and wellness," said Mario Kahn, vice president, Toyo Bio-Pharma. "Our cosmeceutical ingredients often draw on ancient historic beauty uses, but are also backed by modern scientific support.

"Cosmeceuticals combine the best of both worlds: wellness and beauty, ancient traditions, and new science." At this intersection, marketers are seeking to help define the term "cosmeceutical." Karen E. Todd, R.D., director of marketing, Kyowa Hakko USA Inc., said the term tends to imply a product that is neither a drug, nor a cosmetic, but one that has a desired impact inside the skin. And Doug Lynch, vice president of sales and marketing, Unigen USA, agreed there are inherent expectations in this area. "To product developers, it has come to mean any nutritional supplement that demonstrably improves health and beauty, with a particular focus on skin health," he said.

The Appeal of Natural Ingredients

Ron Udell, president, Soft Gel Technologies Inc. (SGTI), agreed the term "cosmeceutical" may have initially encompassed topical formulation but has expanded. "Initially, the term referred to topical cosmetics that contained functional ingredients," he said. "Large, mainstream cosmetic companies and a few natural products companies were including traditional dietary supplement ingredients, such as coenzyme Q10 [CoQ10] and green tea catechins, in their formulas—similar to the way food companies were adding those ingredients into food formulations and creating 'functional foods.' As a nutrition company first, SGTI defines cosmeceutials in the strictest sense. To us, a cosmeceutical is a product or formula that contains an important nutritional component such as an herb, mineral, or functional dietary nutrient that is ingested for the specific health benefits and appearance of the consumer."

And the appeal of "natural" is certainly helping the growth of the market. "From what the past few years have indicated, consumers show a strong leaning toward the natural versus the synthetic, especially if the natural may work just as well or better," said Blake Ebersole, marketing director, Verdure. "Consumers are starting to understand, at least on a basic level, what researchers have been seeing for years—components that protect the plant, and the mechanisms by which they do this, are frequently the same as that which protect the human."

It is this interest in nutrition supporting both internal health and outward appearance that is helping drive consumer awareness. "More recently, consumers appear to understand that what they eat also plays an important role in how they look," said Barbara Apps, director of business development and marketing, Aloecorp. "As a result, we're seeing functional foods positioned for their skin and beauty benefits, such as yogurt with aloe vera, which has been introduced in Europe and Asia."

Adding to the drive is the increased focus on men's personal care. The Natural Marketing Institute (NMI) said it's "Reigning Men," in its 2007 Trends Report. NMI noted men's personal care is the fastest growing segment in the bath and body care category, driven by what they called "The Massification of Metrosexuals," which allows a broad range of men across demographic and generational lines to explore product offerings. Apps agreed with NMI's assessment, and added, "Men are realizing that their health and appearance can enhance their success in many aspects of life."

Obviously, then, the market for cosmeceuticals is expanding rapidly. Lakshmi Prakash, vice president of innovation and business development, Sabinsa Cosmetics, cited market research showing the cosmeceuticals market, including skin care, makeup, and hair care products, will surpass $17 billion by 2010. She added, "At $7 billion in 2005, skin care, such as anti-aging creams, microdermabrasion home kits and wrinkle remedies, is the largest segment."

An Alternative to Aging

The emphasis on the anti-aging skin care sector is almost to be expected, given the aging boomer population. In addition, Yasuko Kuroda, vice president, Fuji Health Science Inc., said, "The consumer is recently becoming more interested in products that could help them to achieve their cosmetic goals without surgery or treatment with harsh chemicals."

Udell noted it's not just the boomers who are driving interest. "People live longer and are not willing to accept the natural signs of aging—they are seeking the proverbial 'fountain of youth' and are willing to spend hard-earned dollars on natural anti-aging moisturizers and supplements that may erase those fine lines that crop up over time," he said. "And the Generation-X, 30-something consumers are striving to maintain their youthful looks. They are spending thousands of dollars on cosmetic products and procedures to help reverse, or at least suspend, the aging process."

Those cosmetic procedures, however, do come with their risks. "So many mainstream beauty treatments today utilize harsh chemicals and can cause negative side effects," Kahn said. "From Botox to parabens, consumers are increasingly aware of the hazards involved in everything from medispa treatments to hand lotion. They want effective beauty treatments, but, understandably, they don't want the dangers. Cosmeceuticals have therefore entered the market at the perfect time, with such a growing interest in solutions that are both effective and natural."

Bob Capelli, vice president sales and marketing, Cyanotech, said natural cosmeceuticals really came onto the market in the 1990s, but are on the cutting edge in today's personal care arena. "Even mainstream cosmetic companies are looking for natural actives to incorporate into their formulas, basically because consumers want the products they put on their skin to be as natural as possible."

Of course, as consumers seek "natural" ingredients, they are also expecting the products to be both efficacious and safe. Lynch noted suppliers therefore have to take steps to ensure this is the case. "There are risks with being all-natural, namely microbial contamination risk, ensuring consistent supply, and fluctuating pricing pressures," he said. Unigen has addressed the concerns by vertically integrating its operations, purchasing farmland for growing its botanicals to control the soil and prevent contamination. The company can harvest at peak season to ensure consistency and efficacy, and produce the extracts under close watch.

Topical Opportunity

"There are several natural ingredients common in cosmeceutical products: spice extracts as aroma constituents, gums for modifying viscosity, fruit acids for pH adjustment, vegetable oils as emollients and vehicles, waxes as thickeners and emollients, plant extracts as conditioners, and vitamins and fatty acids as moisturizers and antioxidants," Prakash said. However, there are challenges in incorporating natural compounds into topical formulations without compromising the activity. "Aesthetics is a particularly important concern," she said. "For example, a color that is too dark, a gritty texture or dispersibility problems could render the 'healthy and natural' ingredient unattractive. Uptake of actives from formulations is another concern." Sabinsa offers a full range of clinically studied cosmeceutical compounds, including its branded natural extract, Cosmoperine, that improves the uptake and permeation of other co-formulated actives.

Aloe vera is a natural compound that has been used for centuries for its skin health benefits, and has been shown in a more recent study to serve as a carrier of topical ingredients into the skin and tissues, increasing efficacy, according to Apps. "This is in addition to its roles as a detoxifying/antioxidant ingredient, immuno-regulatory ingredient that helps the skin and immune system recover from negative impact of UV [ultraviolet] light, and compound that helps the skin to counteract its lack of resilience and tone from natural, age-related loss of collagen and reinforce the skin's supportive network for a firmer look."

Antioxidants also play a key role in the cosmeceutical market. "Many natural skin care manufacturers are adding antioxidants to their facial creams and moisturizers, such as grapeseed extract, green tea, CoQ10, alpha lipoic acid, vitamin C, lycopene and other botanicals, vitamins and minerals that act as 'natural age fighters,'" Udell said. "More Americans are becoming aware of the antioxidant and moisturizing properties of these natural ingredients."

There is some research on the use of topical antioxidants for skin health. Topical application of vitamins C and E has shown significant photoprotection against UV damage, possibly by scavenging reactive oxygen species. Used topically, C and E may also be able to reverse mottled pigmentation and photoaging-related wrinkles.

Carotenoids also offer antioxidant support to the skin. Topical application of lycopene, for example, was found in one study to significantly reverse UVB-induced photodamage. And in vitro work with an astaxanthin-rich algal extract found the compound could protect against UVA-induced DNA alterations in human skin cells.

"Astaxanthin is the world's strongest antioxidant and is also a safe, natural antiinflammatory," Capelli said. "Some companies are putting our BioAstin astaxanthin into rejuvenating and anti-aging skin creams, while another company is putting it into a line of natural lipsticks. Four different sunscreen manufacturers are also putting BioAstin into sunscreen products and marketing them as 'anti-aging' formulas."

Another powerful antioxidant with cosmeceutical benefits is pine bark extract. Frank Schonlau, Ph.D., director of scientific communications, Natural Health Science, stated: "Pycnogenol French maritime pine bark extract is an evidence-based product, and its benefits as a cosmeceutical stem from its selective binding affinity to collagen and elastin. Pycnogenol in-

Biophysical Tests Can Gain Trust

As anti-aging product claims grow bolder every day, marketers face challenges from public health and government agencies, consumer and advertising watchdogs, and competitors. Claims must be supported by objective biophysical tests that are combined with consumer perception, clinical, safety, and toxicology studies. To avoid regulatory or legal action, it is advisable to support each claim. Biophysical methods usually adequately support performance claims, and while these evaluations have not been standardized, their results are usually accepted because they are based on sound scientific principles and hence, are considered adequate for supporting claims. These biophysical evaluations are further strengthened by clinical evaluations by trained technicians and dermatologists.

Navin M. Geria,
"Clinical Studies Reveal Cosmeceuticals' Benefits,"
Entrepreneur, *October 2007.*

hibits destruction of collagen and elastin by oxidative stress such as during sunburn and also from degenerative enzymes in the skin." . . .

The Science of Age Reversal

Skin nourishing products must deliver benefits from the epidermis through the dermal and sub-cutaneous connective layers. Michael Wang, product manager, NuLiv Science USA, noted oxidation from pollution or UV radiation has been linked to decreased collagen biosynthesis in the skin's dermal layers, leading to sagging, wrinkling, and a general loss of tone. "For skin to look young and firm, sufficient amounts of collagen in the skin are critical," he said. "There are two ways to accomplish this: increase the biosynthesis of collagen or inhibit the decomposition of existing collagen in the dermal layer."

Formulators are therefore looking to specialty compounds that can help in this fight. Among the possibilities Wang cited were proline to assist collagen biosynthesis, the polysaccharide hyaluronic acid (HA) for lubrication, and compounds to inhibit matrix metalloproteinases (MMPs), the enzyme responsible for decomposing collagen.

NuLiv has conducted in-house studies on its Astrion patent-pending botanical extract, and has found it may enhance proline absorption and HA biosynthesis, and inhibit collagen decomposition. The company also conducted a small-scale human study that found ASTRION application could reduce wrinkles by 20 percent and melanin by 22 percent, leading to a lightening effect.

Kyowa Hakko has also developed a specialty ingredient, Resilen-200, a low-molecular-weight HA, that may help increase penetration of actives into the skin and support HA biosynthesis. Todd noted, "The main challenge in formulating cosmeceuticals is delivering actives into the skin in proper levels to ensure activity." The company also supplies Lhydroxyproline, as Lumistor, and holds several patents on the use of hydroxyproline and N-acetylhydroxyproline derivatives or salts in combination with water-soluble or oil-soluble vitamins.

Another ingredient with specific skin benefits is pomegranate. "Published research indicates topical benefits with several parts of the pomegranate-fruit, including seed components," Ebersole said, noting Verdure recently released a cosmeceutical ingredient, Pu nicinol-5 made from 100 percent pomegranate and standardized to 80 percent essential fatty acids (EFAs) and 75 percent punicic acid. . . .

Expanding the Market

The largest organ of the body, the skin is an external manifestation of internal health and wellness. For years, consumers have tried detoxification regimens or ingested compounds from silica to vitamin C to improve the appearance of the skin. The growing market for "cosmeceuticals" has a significant crossover into the ingestibles area.

"There's a lot of potential for the cosmeceutical world, whether as a whole health and beauty supplement or topical treatment," Kahn said. "And we're also seeing a lot of interest in combining the two—both topical and oral—to intensify benefits."

Capelli noted Cyanotech has seen greater interest in combination systems. "Astaxanthin is proven to protect the skin from UV light damage both when applied topically as well as when taken internally, so we have a few companies that are considering developing an inside-out, two product system," he said.

Kuroda echoed the sentiment, adding Fuji Health Science has a patent pending on the use of internal astaxanthin for wrinkle reduction, and sponsored two human studies to support the application. In a Japanese study, researchers randomized 16 healthy women over age 40, all with dry skin, to receive a supplement of 5-percent astaxanthin (as AstaReal) and palm oil with 37.5-percent vitamin E (as Tocomin, from Carotech). After four weeks, significant improvement was seen in skin moisture content, self-assessment of skin condition, and inspection/palpitation by a cosmetic specialist. Improvement of wrinkles was also noted based on skin observation. A second study, conducted on 49 healthy women in Rockland, Maine (age about 47), provided subjects with a placebo soft gel or one with astaxanthin for six weeks. After intervention, subjects taking astaxanthin had significant improvements in fine lines/wrinkles and elasticity by dermatologist assessment, and in moisture content by instrumental assessment. The researchers suggested astaxanthin may protect fresh collagen from oxidative stress.

Also exploring the synergistic effects of internal and external nutrition is SGTI, which Udell noted looks at cosmeceuticals as encompassing both areas. "While external treatments may provide a more youthful appearance, people need to realize that they are the same age on the inside," he said. To address part of the issue, SGTI supplies several antioxidant ingredients that may help quench free radicals that can accelerate the aging process. "Accumulating evidence strongly suggests oxidative stress is linked to almost every disease of aging," Udell added.

The company also markets Injuv, a 9-percent, low molecular weight HA dietary supplement in a soft gelatin capsule for softening skin. "Supplementation with Injuv can increase the HA content throughout the body, including the dermis," Udell said. "HA exists in both the dermis and epidermis, therefore Injuv moisturizes from the deeper layer to the upper layer." In a company-supported clinical trial conducted in Japan on 96 women, ages 22 to 65 years, Injuv increased skin smoothness and firmness.

Whether delivering cosmeceuticals orally, topically or synergistically, suppliers note there is great opportunity for companies that develop effective products that can meet consumer expectations. "Buyers should be sure they understand the marketability of the finished product—what will trigger consumers to actually buy the product," Capelli said. "Buying a cutting-edge, natural, efficacious nutraceutical to put in a cosmeceutical product is certainly the best way to go."

Udell concluded: "It is difficult for the natural products industry to compete with cosmetic surgeons and dermatologists who administer Botox treatments and facial peels, because these are both highly visible industries whose results are seen weekly on makeover 'reality' shows. However, for those individuals who are not looking to undertake such 'extreme' measures to change their appearance and fight aging, the natural health industry can provide alternatives."

> *"The solid evidence that cosmeceuticals work is scant; published research on specific product formulations is practically nonexistent."*

Many Cosmeceuticals Tout Misleading Claims

Erika Kawalek

"Cosmeceuticals" are cosmetics that are advertised or alleged to have pharmaceutical benefits. In the following viewpoint, Erika Kawalek contends that this class of expensive beauty products, which promises to erase wrinkles and fine lines or make the skin more youthful, often does not deliver. However, even with their scientific-sounding ingredients and medical endorsements, the author maintains that the safety and efficacy of cosmeceuticals are not closely regulated in the United States as true drugs are. Consequently, cosmetic companies are free to use all but a few banned chemicals and market products with unsubstantiated claims, Kawalek argues. The author is associate director of the New York Institute for the Humanities at New York University.

As you read, consider the following questions:

1. What ingredients does the author list as commonly found in cosmeceuticals?

Erika Kawalek, "Artfully Made-up," *Legal Affairs*, November–December 2005. Reproduced by permission.

2. What happened in the Lash Lure incident, according to Kawalek?

3. As stated in the viewpoint, why is cosmetics regulation not a high priority?

Last December [2004], Debra Scheufler, a 47-year-old attorney from San Diego, gave up on Crème de la Mer, the $110-per-ounce anti-aging face cream with a cultish following. The moisturizer had been part of her morning and nighttime beauty regimen for about four months. But it didn't make her skin "softer, firmer . . . virtually creaseless," as the cream's promotional materials had promised. "Aging lines" were not "noticeably less visible." Her complexion got worse. "My skin was getting clogged and it wasn't looking any younger," she said. "Fine lines were not going away." After looking up the ingredients in a cosmetics dictionary, Scheufler discovered that Crème de la Mer was composed mostly of petrolatum (essentially Vaseline), mineral oil, seaweed extract, and a handful of antioxidants, vitamins, and minerals—in about the same proportions as less expensive creams.

She filed a class action suit against Estée Lauder, Inc., which owns the brand La Mer among others, and against cosmetics companies like L'Oréal and Procter & Gamble that also manufacture and promote anti-aging skin care products. On grounds of false advertising and unfair competition, Scheufler is seeking reimbursement for herself, in the amount of $500 to $1,000, and for other women and men who believe they've been defrauded by the "anti-aging" claims on cosmetics. "These are cosmetics, but they would have consumers think they have medical uses and benefits," said Howard Rubinstein, one of her lawyers.

Above Accountability Laws

In today's marketplace, making an informed decision about cosmetics is difficult, in spite of the law that requires ingredients to be listed in descending order of amount, according to guidelines established by the United States Food and Drug Administration [FDA]. Called the Fair Packaging and Labeling Act [FPLA] and passed in 1966, the law came about after decades of industry negligence and a burst of consumer activism. Consumers wanted to know what chemicals they were slathering on their bodies. They wanted to keep exaggerated claims about the benefits of a product in check.

In the generation since, the cosmetics industry has repeatedly looked for ways to boost its revenues and circumvent the costs of regulation. At times, the FDA and the Federal Trade Commission have successfully enforced the FPLA and related consumer-protection laws. But as Scheufler and others are discovering, the watchdogs at those agencies are struggling to combat increased challenges from the industry and to live with budget cuts and the government's relatively laissez-faire attitude.

The latest unsubstantiated claims (and, perhaps, unsafe products) made by cosmetics firms come in the form of "cosmeceuticals"—cosmetics packed with extra ingredients, like Alpha Hydroxy Acids, Ester-C, and copper peptides said to have therapeutic benefits. They are taking up increasing amounts of counter space at Saks Fifth Avenue, Wal-Mart, and other outlets, as well as air time on the QVC television shopping network. The solid evidence that cosmeceuticals work is scant; published research on specific product formulations is practically nonexistent. Anyone can slap a "ceutical" on a product as easily as he can add "dermatologist-tested," "hypoallergenic," "noncomedogenic," and "all natural."

But many cosmeceuticals look, sound, feel—and cost—a lot like drugs or other FDA-approved therapies. They are often created with pharmacological- or scientific-sounding ingredients and are endorsed by doctors like the mediagenic Nicholas Perricone. This allows the cosmetics companies to price and sell cosmeceuticals like drugs—at $110 per ounce, for example—but because of the FDA's limited resources and its bifurcation of the substances it regulates into drugs and cosmetics, the companies are able to avoid the costly testing and monitoring that a true drug requires.

Thriving from Neglect

The industry is thriving from that neglect. According to an estimate from the market research company Packaged Facts, cosmeceutical skin-care products took in more than $6.4 billion domestically in 2004. That's more than half of the $12.4 billion for all cosmeceuticals, an amount that is expected to increase to over $16 billion by 2010. About half of all skin-care cosmeceuticals belong to the category of anti-aging creams, a vague category for a class of products that promises to reduce wrinkles, plump skin, promote cell renewal, boost collagen, and expose new skin, among other benefits.

The popularity of cosmeceuticals is growing in tandem with the demand for plastic surgery and dermatological procedures. In 2004, 9.2 million cosmetic surgery procedures were performed, contributing to an $8.4 billion industry that has grown by 25 percent since 2000. The most popular techniques are the least invasive ones—Botox injections, chemical peels, and microdermabrasion.

Cosmeceuticals target consumers who are leery of plastic surgery and who want to prevent the need for future surgery, which includes almost all of us. Many product inserts and advertisements, like a well-known ad for Basic Research's StriVectin-SD, imply "Better than Botox" results; others, like an ad for Dior's Capture, offer an "Alternative to a Facelift." Cosmetics companies are racing to unveil products that sound effective and up-to-the-minute, employing the latest buzzwords of the medical establishment. "We've had a lot of clients who want to say 'manufactured in a pharmaceutical laboratory,'" said Richard Morey, a partner with the Washington, D.C., law firm of Kleinfeld, Kaplan & Becker. "It's the aura that you want to give a product, because everybody knows that drugs really work whereas cosmetics are puffery." Lately, the buzz has been about Nicholas Perricone's Alpha Lipoic Acid with Tocotrienols, which purports to reduce spider veins. In a few months, the buzz will be about something else.

Confusion abounds. What is Alpha Lipoic Acid with Tocotrienols, and how much of this stuff do we need to fade spider veins? Are the few cosmeceutical studies that exist scientifically sound? And are cosmeceuticals safe to use with other products? "The intelligent Harvard graduate with a Ph.D. can't make a sensible choice when she goes in and looks for a good moisturizer," said Dr. Albert Kligman, the University of Pennsylvania dermatologist who coined the term "cosmeceutical" 25 years ago [in 1980] to refer to a class of creams that does more than decorate or camouflage and less than treat a disease. Despite the presumed skepticism of consumers—cosmetics companies defend themselves by saying that consumers know companies rely on hyperbole and illusion to promote sales—the industry has made believers out of most of the public. An April 2004 survey conducted by the National Consumers League revealed that 6 out of 10 adults think that the FDA tests anti-aging products for safety and efficacy. It does no such thing.

Consumer Tragedies

Until the early 1900s, American women brewed cosmetics in their kitchens. They used ingredients gleaned from the pantry, the farm, the garden, and, occasionally, the local druggist. Most of them learned how to make these concoctions from recipe books that made little distinction among treating the flu, stuffing a turkey, or smoothing a brow. Lard, rosewater, and coconut milk made a pleasing hand cream for Sarah Joseph Hale, the editor of *Godey's Lady's Book*, a popular 19th-century magazine. What was her anti-aging treatment? Soaking brown butcher's paper in apple vinegar before applying it to her forehead. The remedy likely contained alpha hydroxy acids, present in fruit sugars, which peeled a layer of her skin (exfoliated it), giving it a softer look.

Anti-aging products gained popularity on a mass level in the 1920s, when young women attempted to replicate the boyish figures and faces of men who had been killed in battle, explained historian Fenja Gunn in *The Artificial Face*. The quest for youth "encouraged beauty salons to produce a range of preparations and treatments designed to erase wrinkles, discourage double chins and generally preserve a youthful complexion." As women entered the workforce in greater numbers and migrated to the city, they began to purchase cosmetics more widely. In addition to the pleasures of grooming, cosmetics seemed to offer users a competitive advantage in both the career and mating markets.

In 1933, a woman known as Mrs. Brown made a trip to Byrd's Beauty Shoppe in Dayton, Ohio. A beautician encouraged her to try a popular eyelash dye called Lash Lure. That night Mrs. Brown was being honored for her volunteer work with the local PTA [Parent-Teacher Association] and, wanting to look her finest, she opted for the treatment. Almost immediately, her eyes itched and burned. *The New Republic* described her terrible morning after: "Her eyes are gone and the flesh around them is a mass of tortured scars."

The Lash Lure incident capped a series of consumer tragedies. Dozens of women were crippled or poisoned because of a depilatory called Kormelu. The American Medical Association released evidence that Kormelu contained rat poison. That's when the National Consumers League and doctors began to lobby for FDA regulation of the beauty industry. Books like *American Chamber of Horrors, Skin Deep*, and *100,000,000 Guinea Pigs* lambasted the government's lax stance about food, drug, and cosmetics manufacturers and they raised awareness about the dangers posed by use of unregulated products.

Selling Miracle Ingredients Without Results

Angel dusting, also known as fairy dusting or window dressing, is an unfortunately common practice in the cosmetics, cosmeceuticals, and dietary supplement industries. In formulating a product, certain suspect manufacturers incorporate a miniscule portion of an active ingredient, insufficient to produce any measurable benefit, for the sole purpose of deceiving consumers. By including even trace amounts of an active substance in a particular formula, marketers can make sweeping claims about its benefits without any evidence of results.

Truthinaging.com,
"What Is It: Angel Dusting," March 24, 2009.

Bad Behavior Is Still Common in the Cosmetics Industry

In 1938, Congress stepped in to pass the Food, Drug, and Cosmetic Act. The law extended the FDA's jurisdiction to include cosmetics, defined as "articles intended to be rubbed, poured, sprinkled, or sprayed on, introduced into, or otherwise applied to the human body . . . for promoting attractiveness." In contrast, drugs were defined as "articles intended for the use in diagnosis, cure, mitigation, treatment, or prevention of disease" or that are "intended to affect the structure or any function of the body of man."

This question of intent is paramount because a drug—any product claiming to affect the structure of the body, regardless of what its ingredients are—must be reviewed by the FDA for safety and efficacy before it's sold on the market. Drug companies must report all complaints about drugs they make and market, and they must adhere to strict manufacturing processes. In other words, drugs must deliver the benefits they claim to, while doing no harm. Even products intended to be used as both a cosmetic and a drug are supposed to have their drug claims and ingredients regulated as drugs. For example, anti-dandruff shampoo must be labeled with the active anti-dandruff ingredient, and the ingredient must be tested before going on the market or have been previously recognized as safe and effective for the intended use.

Cosmetics, on the other hand, are produced, tested, labeled, marketed, and sold without any FDA supervision. With the exception of nine banned ingredients like mercury compounds and chloroform and a list of color additives, cosmetics firms can use any ingredients they want. They are also effectively free to make outsized claims about their products. The FDA has the right to inspect a factory, request a label change, and seize a product it deems dangerous or wrongly branded, but only after the questionable product has been brought to market—and has caught a regulator's eye.

Because they are so loosely regulated, cosmetics companies are supposed to refrain from making drug-like claims about their products. The director of the FDA's Office for Cosmetics and Colors, Dr. Linda Katz, puts this plainly: "If a manufacturer is making labeling claims that would make a cosmetic a drug, it is a drug. And it would need to go through the drug side for testing." If the FDA found that the maker of a cosmeceutical claimed that its product performed like a drug, the company could be penalized for distributing a misbranded or unapproved drug. Still, most companies are willing to take the risk of FDA censure because their chances of getting caught are slim. Even if they are apprehended, by the time the FDA receives a consumer complaint, sends off a series of warning letters, or issues a summons for an injunction, years might have passed. As in other industries, larger companies seem to prefer to pay fines as a cost of doing business and to continue with the bad behavior. With the increased medicalization of beauty, therapeutic claims are too profitable to pass up.

By stretching the limits of traditional claims about cosmetics and as a result of limited resources at the FDA, the cosmeceutical industry has avoided the much more costly process of getting its products approved as drugs. The drug side of the FDA, the Center for Drug Evaluation and Research, won't even talk about cosmeceuticals—the center declined to have a representative interviewed for this article and referred interested parties back to Katz.

The FDA Set a Fleeting Precedent

The FDA has not always been as permissive. Laura Heymann, an assistant professor at William & Mary School of Law, reported that in the 1960s, for example, the FDA challenged cosmetics manufacturers that produced creams promising to smooth out wrinkles. The agency went to court numerous times against the manufacturers of Sudden Change and Line Away, creams that were composed of bovine albumin and water and, when applied to the face, that dried like filmy egg whites and temporarily tightened wrinkles.

The U.S. Court of Appeals for the Second Circuit held that, because Sudden Change advertised itself as a "Face Lift Without the Surgery" and because the manufacturer claimed that the product would "lift out puffs," it should be designated a drug. Likewise, the Third Circuit held that phrases like "super-active," "amazing protein lotion," and "tightening the skin" in Line Away's advertising materials implied that the product was therapeutic rather than cosmetic in nature, and that it should be regulated as a drug. Statements that Line Away was made in a "pharmaceutical laboratory" and packaged under "biologically aseptic conditions" implied that the product itself was a pharmaceutical. "When 'puffery' contains the strong therapeutic implications we find in the Line Away promotional material," the court stated, "we think the dividing line has been crossed." After the 1969 Third Circuit ruling, the manufacturers were forced to change their labeling or face further injunctions against sales and seizures of the products. They complied, and the products soon faded from the marketplace.

By the early 1980s, though, the cosmetics companies were at it again. In 1986, Dr. Christiaan Barnard, the surgeon who two decades before had performed the first heart transplant, co-created and endorsed Glycel, an anti-aging cream made by Alfin Fragrances that contained "glycosphingolipid," an ingredient whose unpronounceability made it seem scientific. He said it possessed "the ability to cause rejuvenation of cells," and women flocked to the beauty counter to buy it.

Estée Lauder and L'Oréal, which for years had been producing anti-aging creams of their own, rushed to label their products with scientific or scientific-sounding terms to compete with the surgeon-endorsed brand. The lotions promised to speed cell turnover, maximize oxygen uptake, strengthen the skin's inner structure, and reverse the effects of aging. Glycel touted "glycosphingolipid," but Estée Lauder responded with lotions containing "Cellular Recovery Complex."

In 1987, Daniel Michels, the director of the Office of Compliance for the FDA's Center for Drugs and Biologics, determined that the companies had gone too far. He issued warning letters to 23 cosmetics firms requesting that they cease making what he called structure/function claims. Claims about "cell rejuvenation," for example, would no longer be tolerated because they promised to affect the structure of the skin. That meant rewriting brochures and text on packaging, in addition to changing the products' advertisements. If the companies didn't respond, they risked product seizures, injunctions against sales, and lawsuits. The companies complied, and the FDA had the funds and political backing to keep them in check—for a while.

Too Busy to Keep Pace

The 1938 act requires the FDA to regulate cosmetics in order to protect consumers from injurious substances and economic harm. But the FDA has not kept up with the profusion of cosmeceuticals. "In my review, these regulatory gaps raise serious questions about the FDA's ability to effectively oversee the cosmetics industry in this country," said Senator Ron Wyden, the Democrat from Oregon, at a 1989 hearing about the potential health hazards of cosmetics products—and the story hasn't changed much since then.

Occasionally, the FDA issues warnings to manufacturers. In January [2005], it sent one such letter to Basic Research, the marketer and distributor of StriVectin-SD and other products. "This letter is in reference to your firm's marketing and distribution of StriVectin-SD, StriVectin-SD Eye Cream, Dermalin-Apg, Mamralin-Ara, and TestroGel," the letter, written by FDA District Director B. Belinda Collins, reads. Some of the drug claims referred to in the letter include, "Clinically Proven to Dramatically Reduce the Appearance of Existing Stretch Mark Length, Depth, Texture, and Discoloration"; "Optimum Glycosaminoglycan and Collagen Synthesis"; "Better than Botox?"; and "Superior wrinkle-reducing properties of a patented oligo-peptide. . . ." The list names nearly 40 other drug claims for Basic Research products, 11 of which pertain to StriVectin-SD. But this censure seems ineffective: According to one industry consultant, StriVectin-SD's earnings will reach over $100 million in 2005, a sign of FDA inaction and consumer confusion. For every FDA warning letter, thousands of misbranded cosmetics, especially anti-aging creams, slip by. The annual growth rate in the sales of anti-aging creams is 11 percent. As with all cosmetics, "If it's a cosmeceutical, you don't have to do a damn thing to prove that it works or that it's safe," Dr. Kligman explained. "There is no regulation whatsoever. You can get a bucket, mix it up in your basement, and put your name on it and sell it."

Despite the potential health risks of cosmeceuticals and the misbranding of products done by this anything-goes industry, the FDA is too busy to keep pace. "The FDA has higher priorities today—bioterrorism, including securing the food supply, and drug safety, both the drug approval process and post-approval monitoring," said Susan Brienza, a Denver-based attorney with the law firm of Patton Boggs LLP, who specializes in cosmetics regulation law and advises clients on issues such as labeling requirements. Richard Cleland, who monitors advertising practices at the Federal Trade Commission [FTC], which works in consort with the FDA to monitor advertising practices, agreed: "Cosmetics, in terms of enforcement priorities, tend not to be as high." The FDA and FTC, he explained, are more likely to go after dietary supplements and bogus cancer cures than anti-aging creams, because supplements might harm people and bogus cures might prevent them from seeking proper medical care.

It's logical that the FDA is choosing to focus on potentially harmful or life-altering drugs rather than anti-aging creams. But by doing so, it is ignoring a primary purpose of the 1938 act—to protect the economic interests of consumers. The current regulatory scheme leaves consumers like Debra Scheufler with little recourse. Her case is unlikely to be certified as a class action, but from her point of view it's worth pursuing because the suit has raised public awareness about cosmeceuticals, which raises the chance she will be reimbursed by Estée Lauder. "The manufacturers know that if they go to court, the chances are about 90 percent that they'll lose," Richard Morey said. For that reason, and to avoid bad publicity, the companies usually settle injury and false advertising complaints out of court.

In the meantime, Scheufler is taking inventory of her medicine cabinet, relying on a cosmetics dictionary to help her cut through the pseudoscience. Her latest anti-aging treatment is to work out five days a week and stay out of the sun.

> *"Psychologists and eating-disorder experts . . . say the fashion industry has gone too far in pushing a dangerously thin image that women, and even very young girls, may try to emulate."*

The Fashion Industry May Be Linked to Poor Body Image and Eating Disorders

Nanci Hellmich

In the following viewpoint, Nanci Hellmich claims that the progression of fashion models to extreme thinness may be warping women's and girls' body images. According to the author, concerned health professionals and eating-disorder experts have come forward, asserting that repeated exposure to unnaturally skinny models—in magazines, catalogs, and television shows—feeds body dissatisfaction, which can lead to anorexia, bulimia, and other harmful weight-control behaviors. While professionals in fashion and modeling claim to work with only healthy models, Hellmich suggests that the media take responsibility for representing women of all sizes. Hellmich is a reporter for USA Today.

Nanci Hellmich, "Do Thin Models Warp Girls' Body Image?" *USA Today*, September 25, 2006. Reproduced by permission.

As you read, consider the following questions:

1. According to Spain's ban, what is considered a healthy model?

2. As stated by Hellmich, what percentage of girls can resist unhealthy body images?

3. How does Kelly Cutrone describe models?

When Frederique van der Wal, a former Victoria's Secret model, attended designers' shows during New York's Fashion Week this month [September 2006], she was "shocked" by the waiflike models who paraded down the catwalk. They seemed even skinnier than in previous years.

"This unnatural thinness is a terrible message to send out. The people watching the fashion shows are young, impressionable women," says van der Wal, host of *Cover Shot* on TLC.

Psychologists and eating-disorder experts are worried about the same thing. They say the fashion industry has gone too far in pushing a dangerously thin image that women, and even very young girls, may try to emulate.

"We know seeing super-thin models can play a role in causing anorexia," says Nada Stotland, professor of psychiatry at Rush Medical College in Chicago and vice president of the American Psychiatric Association. Because many models and actresses are so thin, it makes anorexics think their emaciated bodies are normal, she says. "But these people look scary. They don't look normal."

The widespread concern that model thinness has progressed from willowy to wasted has reached a threshold as evidenced by the recent actions of fashion show organizers.

The Madrid [Spain] fashion show, which ended Saturday, banned overly thin models, saying it wanted to project beauty and health. Organizers said models had to be within a healthy weight range.

That means a 5-foot-9 woman would need to weigh at least 125 pounds.

Officials in India, Britain and Milan also have expressed concerns, but some experts say consumers in the USA will have to demand models with fuller figures for it to happen here.

The Impact on Impressionable Women

"The promotion of the thin, sexy ideal in our culture has created a situation where the majority of girls and women don't like their bodies," says body-image researcher Sarah Murnen, professor of psychology at Kenyon College in Gambier, Ohio. "And body dissatisfaction can lead girls to participate in very unhealthy behaviors to try to control weight."

Experts call these behaviors disordered eating, a broad term used to describe a range of eating problems, from frequent dieting to anorexia nervosa (which is self-starvation, low weight and fear of being fat) to bulimia nervosa (the binge-and-purge disorder).

Girls today, even very young ones, are being bombarded with the message that they need to be super-skinny to be sexy, says psychologist Sharon Lamb, co-author of *Packaging Girlhood: Rescuing Our Daughters from Marketers' Schemes*.

It used to be that women would only occasionally see rail-thin models, such as Twiggy, the '60s fashion icon. "But now they see them every day. It's the norm," Lamb says, from ads, catalogs and magazines to popular TV shows such as *America's Next Top Model* and *Project Runway*. "They are seeing skinny models over and over again."

On top of that, gaunt images of celebrities such as Nicole Richie and Kate Bosworth are plastered on magazine covers, she says.

What worries Lamb most is that these images are filtering down to girls as young as 9 and 10. Some really sexy clothes are available in children's size 6X, says Lamb, a psychology professor at Saint Michael's College in Colchester, Vermont. "Girls are being taught very young that thin and sexy is the way they want to be when they grow up, so they'd better start working on that now," she says.

Lamb believes it's fine for girls to want to feel sexy and pretty when they are teenagers, but that shouldn't be their primary focus. "If they are spending all their time choosing the right wardrobe, trying to dance like an MTV backup girl and applying lip gloss, it robs them of other options."

Some girls don't want to participate in sports because they're afraid they'll bulk up. Some won't try to play an instrument such as a trombone because it doesn't fit their image of what a "girly girl" should do, she says.

It Begins in Youth

There's no question younger girls are getting this message, says Murnen, who has studied this for 15 years. "We have done studies of grade-school girls, and even in grade 1, girls think the culture is telling them that they should model themselves after celebrities who are svelte, beautiful, and sexy."

Some girls can reject that image, but it's a small percentage: 18% in Murnen's research. Those girls were shown to have the highest body esteem. Murnen and her colleagues reviewed 21 studies that looked at the media's effect on more than 6,000 girls, ages 10 and older, and found those who were exposed to the most fashion magazines were more likely to suffer from poor body images.

Societies throughout the ages have had different ideals for female beauty, says Katie Ford, chief executive officer of Ford Models, whose megastar models include Christie Brinkley and Rachel Hunter. "You can look as far back as Greek statues and paintings and see that. It's part of women's fantasy nature," Ford says. "The question is: When does that become destructive?"

She doesn't buy into the idea that fashion models are creating a cult of thinness in the USA. "The biggest problem in America is obesity. Both obesity and anorexia stem from numerous issues, and it would be impossible to attribute either to entertainment, be it film, TV, or magazines."

The Anatomy of a Runway Model

This year's fashion shows in New York featured a mix of figure types, some of them a little more womanly and some thin, says Ford, whose agency had about 20 models in shows of top designers, including Ralph Lauren, Bill Blass, Marc Jacobs and Donna Karan. "Our models who did very well this season were not super-skinny. However, there were some on the runway who were very thin."

Cindi Leive, editor in chief of *Glamour* magazine, says some models were teens who hadn't developed their curves yet, which is one reason they appeared so thin. "You do see the occasional model on the runway looking like she should go from the fashion show to the hospital. You hear stories of girls who come to model and are collapsing because they haven't eaten in days. Any responsible model booker will tell you they turn away girls who get too thin."

Runway models have to have a certain look, says Kelly Cutrone, owner of People's Revolution, a company that produces fashion shows around the world. Her company produced 16 fashion shows in New York, including one for designer Marc Bouwer.

The runway models this year were no thinner than years before, she says. "I didn't see any difference in the girls at all. When they bend over, are you going to see the rib cage? Yes, they are thin naturally."

Women shouldn't be comparing themselves with these girls, she says. "These girls are anomalies of nature. They are freaks of nature. They are not average. They are naturally thin and have incredibly long legs compared to the rest of their body. Their eyes are set wide apart. Their cheekbones are high."

Most runway models are 14 to 19, with an average age of 16 or 17, she says. Some are older. Many are 5-foot-10 or 5-foot-11. They average 120 to 124 pounds. They wear a size 2 or 4. "If we get a girl who is bigger than a 4, she is not going to fit the clothes," Cutrone says. "Clothes look better on thin people. The fabric hangs better."

Stephanie Schur, designer of her own line, Michon Schur, had her first official runway show in New York a few weeks ago. When she was casting models, she looked for women who had "a nice glow, a healthy look."

She encountered a few models who looked unhealthy. "They tend to be extremely pale, have thin hair and don't have that glow."

But many of today's runway models look pretty much alike, Schur says. "They are all pretty girls, but no one really stands out. For runway it's about highlighting the clothes. It's finding the girls that make your clothes look best."

Schur says she doesn't believe many young girls today are going to try to imitate what they see on the fashion runways. She says they are more likely to look to actresses for their ideal body image.

It's not surprising that women want to be slender and beautiful, because as a society "we know more about women who look good than we know about women who do good," says Audrey Brashich, a former teen model and author of *All Made Up: A Girl's Guide to Seeing Through Celebrity Hype and Celebrating Real Beauty*.

For several years, Brashich worked for *Sassy* and *YM* magazines and read thousands of letters from girls and teens who wanted to become a famous model, actress, or singer.

And no wonder, she says. "As a culture, we are on a first-name basis with women like Paris Hilton or Nicole Richie," she says. "The most celebrated, recognizable women today are famous primarily for being thin and pretty, while women who are actually changing the world remain comparatively invisible. Most of us have a harder time naming women of other accomplishments." The idolizing of models, stars, and other celebrities is not going to change "until pop culture changes the women it celebrates and focuses on."

Women Come in All Sizes

Glamour's Leive believes the media have a powerful influence on women's body images and a responsibility to represent women of all sizes. "We do not run photos of anybody in the magazine who we believe to be at an unhealthy weight. We frequently feature women of all different sizes. We all know that you can look fabulous in clothes without being a size 2."

Ford believes the trend next year will be to move toward more womanly figures. Model van der Wal agrees and says she's trying to include women of varying figure types in *Cover Shot*. "Women come in lots of different sizes and shapes, and we should encourage and celebrate that."

Cutrone says models will become heavier if that's what consumers demand. "If people decide thin is out, the fashion industry won't have thin models anymore. Have you spent time with fashion people? They are ruthless. They want money.

"And the one thing they know is people want clothes to cover their bodies," Cutrone says. "Unfortunately, most people aren't comfortable with their bodies."

> "Only in America do we think that beauty is a purely natural attribute rather than a type of artistry requiring effort."

Women Can Choose to Follow the Body Image Promoted by the Fashion Industry

Garance Franke-Ruta

Garance Franke-Ruta is a senior editor at the American Prospect *and a fellow at the Joan Shorenstein Center on the Press, Politics and Public Policy. In the following viewpoint, Franke-Ruta opposes the argument that the use of thin models by the fashion industry leads to poor body image and eating disorders. To her, the idea that beauty can be attained without any effort is the real problem, especially in an era of sedentary lifestyles and spreading obesity. Models and celebrities maintain their slim physiques through diet, exercise, and discipline, Franke-Ruta claims, offering that a woman can choose whether attaining beauty is worth the work.*

Garance Franke-Ruta, "The Natural Beauty Myth," *Wall Street Journal*, December 15, 2006. Reprinted with permission of the *Wall Street Journal*.

As you read, consider the following questions:

1. As stated by the author, how do critics view beauty magazines?

2. According to the author, how do attitudes toward beauty differ between Americans and the French?

3. How do media images of beauty help women, in Franke-Ruta's view?

Last week [in December 2006], Italy's government and some of its fashion moguls announced plans to crack down on the use of ultra-thin models on the catwalk. This decision follows in the wake of Madrid's recently instituted ban on underweight models at its annual fashion show. Let's not rush to celebrate. [Editor's note: Italy has banned size zero models.]

Pictures of beautiful but undernourished-looking women have led, in recent months, to a round of fashion-industry bashing in the press. One anonymous wit even mocked up satirical pictures of women who looked like concentration camp victims—except that they had masses of glossy hair and wore slinky clothes. As often happens when satire meets a mass audience, lots of people thought that the doctored pictures were real—which is how, one day in November, they wound up in my inbox, courtesy of a women and media list-serv.

A predictable discussion followed. Curvy women were praised for their healthy-seeming fuller figures. "Self-acceptance" was praised, too. It was argued that the evil images presented to women by the fashion industry were part of the broader plan of beauty magazines to make women feel bad about themselves and thus buy products for self-improvement.

Such a critique, which we hear over and over today, is based on a conceptual error. The beauty industry is not the problem; it is a part of the solution. American women today

Darwinism Demands Skinny Beauty

"'Skinny' has become the most accepted archetype of beauty," said Sarah Musgrave, account director of [global advertising agency] Saatchi & Saatchi in London. "It is youthful; it is aspirational. And when we vilify designers, we have to remember why skinny sells so well—it's Darwinian. We know that—rightly or wrongly—the most beautiful get the mates. Survival of the 'fittest,' if you will, and if we want to ensure our 'survival,' we must appeal not to other women but to men."

Editors, "Skinny Model Furor:
Not All Fashion's Fault, Say Designers (Part 2),"
Women's Wear Daily, January 30, 2007.

are the victims of a more insidious idea, an idea that underlies the American obsession with self-esteem: the tyrannical ideal of "natural beauty."

A "Natural" Life

Few Americans today live a "natural" life, whatever that may be. The more educated and well-to-do among us may eat organic foods and avoid chemicals as best they can, but such efforts hardly make us "natural." Our society is too complex for that. Indeed, all societies involve such a thick layering of culture over our malleable essence that it is virtually impossible to say what we might be like in a natural state.

What is clear is that, over the past century, American women have changed their shape. Most noticeably, they have gained so much poundage that, today, more than half are overweight and a third are clinically obese. The sharpest spike in obesity has come since the late 1970s. There are all sorts of reasons, of course—from the rise of corn syrup as a sweetener to the increased portion sizes of our daily meals and our increasingly sedentary styles of life. And yet the doctrine of "natural beauty"—so favored by the self-esteem brigades of the 1970s and still confusing women today—asks women to accept themselves as this unnatural environment has made them.

What the critics of the beauty industry further fail to recognize is that the doctrine of "natural beauty"—and the desire it breeds in women to be accepted as they are or to be seen as beautiful without any effort—is a ruthless and anti-egalitarian ideal. It is far more punishing than the one that says any woman can be beautiful if she merely treats beauty as a form of discipline.

Only in America do we think that beauty is a purely natural attribute rather than a type of artistry requiring effort. Look at the French: They are no more beautiful as a people than we Americans, but they understand that every woman can be attractive—if not beautiful—if she chooses to be. Yes, we are given forms by nature, but how we choose to present them is a matter of our own discretion. Few people are blessed by nature and circumstance with the Golden Mean proportions that seem to be universally appreciated. Thus, in the end, it is more democratic to think of beauty or attractiveness as an attribute that one can acquire, like speaking a foreign language or cooking well. To see beauty as a capacity like any other—the product of educated taste and daily discipline—is to see it as something chosen: to be possessed or left aside, according to one's preference.

The same goes, relatedly, for maintaining a certain size. In contemporary America, becoming thin is a choice that for most people requires rigorous and sometimes painful self-discipline. But so does becoming a lawyer, or a concert pianist. The celebrity press is wrongly decried for giving women false ideals. In fact, it has demystified the relationship between effort and beauty, between discipline and weight. It opens up a path for non-celebrities.

One celebrity glossy recently estimated that, in a single year, the actress Jennifer Aniston spends close to the average woman's annual salary on trainers and other aspects of a high-level workout. Former tween-queen Britney Spears told Oprah Winfrey that she used to do between 500 and 1,000 crunches a day to perfect her on-display abs. Actress Kate Hudson told one interviewer that, to lose post-pregnancy "baby weight," she worked out three hours a day until she lost her 70 pounds: It was so hard that she used to sit on the exercise cycle and cry. Entertainment figures and models are like athletes; it takes a lot of discipline and social support to look like them. Money helps, too.

Beauty as Something Created

The celebrity magazines also specialize in a genre of stories best understood as tutorials in beauty as artifice: celebrities without their makeup. Makeover shows like *What Not to Wear* and *The Biggest Loser*—even *Queer Eye for the Straight Guy*—show beauty as something created, a condition to which anyone can have access with the right education and effort. This is a meritocratic ideal, not an insistent, elitist one. The makeover shows also help to make it clear that a life of artifice is not for everyone. Once we see the effort and hours that go into making a body more appealing, we may decide not to attempt a labor-intensive presentation of the self. We may decide that other things are more important.

Take, for example, U.S. Navy Commander Sunita L. Williams, an astronaut who recently joined the staff of the International Space Station for six months. Since entering orbit she has announced plans to cut her long chestnut tresses and donate them to charity, because all that hair was uncomfortable and hard to manage in a zero-gravity environment. Most of us live in a less exotic environment, but the essence of our choice is the same. Just as it would be difficult for anyone to be a concert pianist and a nuclear scientist at the same time, it can be a pointless distraction for women to strive to maintain the time-consuming artifices of beauty while pursuing their other goals.

Ms. Williams spent her time in other ways and today has access to the most majestic natural beauty of all: the vision of our globe from space. But it took a half-century of human effort and discipline to put her there.

Periodical Bibliography

*The following articles have been selected to supplement the
diverse views presented in this chapter.*

Alisa Marie Beyer — "You Can Lead a Woman to Nutricosmetics and Cosmeceuticals, But Will She Try Them?" *Global Cosmetic Industry*, November 2008.

Kimberly H. Clancy — "Cosmeceuticals?: The Fine (Regulatory) Line Between Cosmetics and Drugs," *Legal Intelligencer*, June 19, 2008.

Susan Daly — "Now They're Airbrushing the Cover Girls Bigger," *Irish Independent*, June 17, 2009.

Darrin C. Duber-Smith — "No Signs of Aging: Sustained Growth with Cosmeceuticals," *Inside Cosmeceuticals*, October 25, 2007.

Michelle Gillette — "A Company's Ugly Contradiction," *Boston Globe*, November 5, 2007.

Sheila Marikar — "Real? Or Photoshopped? 'Airbrushing' Run Amok," *ABC News*, December 19, 2008.

Jill Nelson — "Dying to Fit the Beauty Standard," *NIA Online*, December 11, 2007.

David Staples — "Fashion Industry Forced to Obey *Vogue*'s Beauty Standards," *Star Phoenix*, June 13, 2007.

Eric Wilson — "In Fashion Magazines, Retouching Stirs a Backlash," *New York Times*, May 28, 2009.

Women's Wear Daily — "Skinny Model Furor: Not All Fashion's Fault, Say Designers, Editors," January 30, 2007.

For Further Discussion

Chapter 1

1. Elizabeth Quil asserts that beauty standards are based on universal, biologically based traits, while Lea Höfel contends that such standards are cultural and historical. In your view, who makes the most compelling argument? Use examples from the viewpoints to support your response.

2. Joanna Briscoe believes that beauty ideals are homogenous, while Christine Lennon suggests they are shifting. Do Briscoe and Lennon promote any notions of beauty that are similar? Use examples from the viewpoints to explain your answer.

Chapter 2

1. Kirsten Anderberg contends that images of beauty are unrealistic and hurt women. Does Linda M. Scott endorse unrealistic ideals of beauty? Explain your response.

2. Jennifer Chamberlain states that the high expectations that come with being physically attractive are a disadvantage in the workplace. Does Gordon L. Patzer successfully address this issue? Use examples from the viewpoints to explain your answer.

Chapter 3

1. Annalisa Barbieri contends that cosmetics help individuals boost their self-esteem. Do you agree with her? Why or why not?

2. Alicia Ouellette argues that cosmetic surgery procedures reduce ethnic characteristics to fit a Caucasian ideal of

beauty. Do the plastic surgery patients Anupreeta Das discusses wish to look white? Use examples from the viewpoints to explain your answer.

Chapter 4

1. Jessica B. Matlin reports that celebrities have replaced models in cosmetics advertising. In your opinion, do stars in such campaigns possess attainable or unrealistic types of beauty? Explain your answer.

2. Erika Kawalek alleges that many cosmeceuticals do not live up to their promises. Does Heather Granato make misleading claims about such products? Use examples from the viewpoints to support your response.

3. Garance Franke-Ruta proposes that celebrities and models who diet and exercise demystify how beauty is achieved and empower women. Do you agree with Franke-Ruta? Why or why not?

Organizations to Contact

The editors have compiled the following list of organizations concerned with the issues debated in this book. The descriptions are derived from materials provided by the organizations. All have publications or information available for interested readers. The list was compiled on the date of publication of the present volume; the information provided here may change. Be aware that many organizations take several weeks or longer to respond to inquiries, so allow as much time as possible.

Academy for Eating Disorders (AED)
111 Deer Lake Road, Suite 100, Deerfield, IL 60015
(847) 498-4274 • fax: (847) 480-9282
e-mail: info@aedweb.org
Web site: www.aedweb.org

Headquartered in Illinois, the AED is an international organization for eating-disorders treatment, research, and education. It provides cutting-edge professional training and education, inspires new developments in eating-disorders research, prevention, and clinical treatments, and is the international source for state-of-the-art information in the field of eating disorders. The AED upholds that the beauty and fashion industries should promote a healthy body image and address eating disorders within the modeling profession.

American Psychological Association (APA)
750 First Street NE, Washington, DC 20002-4242
(800) 374-2721
Web site: www.apa.org

Based in Washington, D.C., APA is a scientific and professional organization that represents psychology in the United States. With 150,000 members, APA is the largest association of psychologists worldwide. It publishes articles and reports on beauty, cosmetic surgery, and other related topics in its numerous journals as well as books, including *The Psychology of Beauty* and *Exacting Beauty: Theory, Assessment, and Treatment of Body Image Disturbance.*

American Society of Plastic Surgeons (ASPS)
444 E. Algonquin Road, Arlington Heights, IL 60005
(847) 228-9900
Web site: www.plasticsurgery.org

ASPS is the largest plastic surgery specialty organization in the world. Established in 1931, it offers patients and consumers information on cosmetic and reconstructive surgery procedures, an online database of plastic surgery statistics, and technology briefs on the latest developments and advances in the field.

Council of Fashion Designers of America (CFDA)
1412 Broadway, Suite 2006, New York, NY 10018
Web site: www.cfda.com

The CFDA is a not-for-profit trade association of more than three hundred of America's foremost fashion and accessory designers. Founded in 1962, the CFDA continues to advance the status of fashion design as a branch of American art and culture, to raise its artistic and professional standards, to define a code of ethical practices of mutual benefit in public and trade relations, and to promote appreciation of the fashion arts through leadership in quality and aesthetic discernment.

Federal Trade Commission (FTC)
Consumer Response Center, 600 Pennsylvania Ave. NW
Washington, DC 20580
(877) 382-4357 (FTC-HELP)
Web site: www.ftc.gov

The FTC deals with issues that touch the economic life of every American. It is the only federal agency with both consumer protection and competition jurisdiction in broad sectors of the economy. The FTC pursues law enforcement; advances consumers' interests by sharing its expertise with federal and state legislatures and U.S. and international government agencies; develops policy and research tools through hearings, workshops, and conferences; and creates practical and plain-language educational programs for consumers and businesses in a global marketplace with constantly changing technologies. The commission monitors the labeling and advertising claims of beauty and personal care products.

Food and Drug Administration (FDA)

5600 Fishers Lane, Rockville, MD   20857
(888) INFO-FDA (463-6332)
Web site: www.fda.org

The FDA is one of the nation's oldest consumer protection agencies. Its mission is to promote and protect the public's health by helping safe and effective products reach the market in a timely way, monitor products for continued safety after they are in use, and help the public get the accurate, science-based information needed to improve health. The FDA provides information on the ingredients and labeling of cosmetics and personal care products.

National Association to Advance Fat Acceptance (NAAFA)

PO Box 22510, Oakland, CA   94609
(916) 558-6880
Web site: www.naafaonline.com

Founded in 1969, NAAFA is a nonprofit civil rights organization dedicated to ending size discrimination in all of its forms. NAAFA's goal is to help build a society in which people of every size are accepted with dignity and equality in all aspects of life. The organization pursues this goal through advocacy, public education, and support.

People for the Ethical Treatment of Animals (PETA)

501 Front Street, Norfolk, VA   23510
(757) 622-PETA (7382) • fax: (757) 622-0457

Web site: www.peta.org

PETA, with more than two million members and supporters, is the largest animal-rights organization in the world. The organization works through public education, cruelty investigations, research, animal rescue, legislation, special events, celebrity involvement, and protest campaigns. It offers a consumer guide to animal-friendly cosmetics, personal care products, and companies.

Personal Care Products Council (PCPC)

1101 17th Street NW, Suite 300
Washington, DC   20036-4702
(202) 331-1770 • fax: (202) 331-1969
Web site: www.personalcarecouncil.org

PCPC (formerly the Cosmetic, Toiletry and Fragrance Association) is a national trade association for the cosmetic and personal care products industry and represents the most innovative names in beauty today. For more than six hundred member companies, the council is the voice on scientific, legal, regulatory, legislative, and international issues for the personal care product industry. PCPC is also a source of information for and about the industry and a vocal advocate for consumer safety and continued access to new products. The council publishes a monthly newsletter and provides consumers with information on cosmetics and personal care products.

Bibliography of Books

John Armstrong   *The Secret Power of Beauty.* New York: Penguin Books, 2005.

Fred E. Basten   *Max Factor: The Man Who Changed the Faces of the World.* New York: Arcade, 2008.

Paula Beguon and Bryan Barron   *Don't Go to the Cosmetics Counter Without Me. 7th ed.* Renton, WA: Beginning Press, 2008.

M. Gigi Durham   *The Lolita Effect: The Media Sexualization of Young Girls and What We Can Do About It.* New York: Overlook Press, 2008.

Umberto Eco, ed.   *History of Beauty.* New York: Rizzoli, 2004.

Umberto Eco, ed.   *On Ugliness.* New York: Rizzoli, 2007.

Anthony Elliot   *Making the Cut: How Cosmetic Surgery Is Transforming Our Lives.* London: Reaktion Books, 2008.

Christine Hoza Farlow   *Dying to Look Good.* Escondido, CA: KISS for Public Health, 2006.

Mary Lisa Gavenas   *Color Stories: Behind the Scenes of America's Billion-Dollar Beauty Industry.* New York: Simon & Schuster, 2007.

Shari Graydon   *In Your Face: The Culture of Beauty and You.* Toronto: Annick Press, 2004.

Dana Heller — *Makeover Television: Realities Remodelled.* New York: Taurus, 2007.

Harold Koda — *Extreme Beauty: The Body Transformed.* New York: Metropolitan Museum of Art, 2004.

Alex Kuczynski — *Beauty Junkies: Inside Our $15 Billion Obsession with Cosmetic Surgery.* New York: Doubleday, 2006.

Don Kulik and Anne Meneley — *Fat: The Anthropology of an Obsession.* New York: Penguin Books, 2005.

Courtney E. Martin — *Perfect Girls, Starving Daughters: The Frightening New Normalcy of Hating Your Body.* New York: Free Press, 2007.

Gordon L. Patzer — *The Power and Paradox of Physical Attractiveness.* Boca Raton, FL: BrownWalker Press, 2006.

Katherine A. Phillips — *Understanding Body Dysmorphic Disorder.* New York: Oxford University Press, 2009.

Jena Pincott — *Do Gentlemen Really Prefer Blondes?: Bodies, Behavior, and Brains—The Science Behind Sex, Love, and Attraction.* New York: Delacorte Press, 2008.

Joanna Pitman — *On Blondes.* New York: Bloomsbury, 2004.

Robert J. Sternberg, ed. — *The Psychology of Love.* New Haven, CT: Yale University Press, 2006.

Elwood Watson and Darcy Martin, eds.

"There She Is, Miss America": The Politics of Sex, Beauty, and Race in America's Most Famous Pageant. New York: Palgrave Macmillan, 2004.

Index